Your Life

Is

Your Business

BUILDING A LIFE OF MOMENTUM

By John Perles and Amy Guy

Momentum Builders Inc.
EFFINGHAM, ILLINOIS 62401

Momentum Builders Inc
PO Box 31
Effingham, Il 62401-0031
http://momentumbuildersinc.com

Ordering Information:
Quantity sales. Special discounts are available on quantity purchases by corporations, associations, and others. For details, contact the "Special Sales Department" at the address above.

Book design by Standoutbooks.com

Your Life Is Your Business/ Momentum Builders Inc. —1st ed.
ISBN 978-0-692-54589-8

CONTENTS

Acknowledgment to my family.

I am what I am because of you. You have taught me, introduced me, challenged me, scolded me, and loved me in ways only you could, and I am so grateful that you continue to. I feel you by my side in my every endeavor. My work matters as you told me it must. Dad promised when he died he would have nothing to leave behind, yet he left the keys and wisdom to all that matters. I have had remarkable advantages in life, which I appreciate and whose demands I will continue to meet.

Love, John Jr.

Your Life Is Your Business

LET ME TELL YOU how I went from where I was to where I am today.

My story is not much different than thousands of others. As I went about navigating my life—learning to overcome obstacles, taking advantage of opportunities, and welcoming rather than fearing new experiences—I gradually adopted strategies and methods that resulted in positive outcomes. This path, which led me to enter the field of strategic planning, is the motivation for my founding of Momentum Builders Inc.

In a manner of speaking, I have come full circle. As I rely on my experiences to help my strategic planning venture grow, I am confident enough in what I have learned to share these tools and insights with individuals on a personal level. In my work, I provide planning protocols for a variety of small and medium-sized businesses. The term *strategic planning* is often met with groans and eye-rolling. However, this process is invaluable to a company and its employees, and it begins with a quick analysis of existing strengths, weaknesses, opportunities, and threats. The information is compiled, two to three objectives are identified, and shorter goals and initiatives are targeted. During this step, it is important to incorporate specific details and date-sensitive commitments. Strategic planning provides a company with a clear look at its business and its capability for building the momentum necessary for continuous growth. I firmly believe the same process works for an individual who is motivated to pursue his or her dreams.

Life Momentum is designed exactly for that purpose. *Your Life Is Your Business* is structured to move you along the path to success in all areas of life. This book offers unique and important principles that, once adopted, will provide a detailed road map for your life's journey. You will discover the benefit of tools to organize and guide your life, and the inspiration to pursue your goals. The road on which you are about to embark is designed to excite you, test you, and ultimately reward you for accepting the challenge.

The Beginning

I WAS ONCE A people watcher. I now am an observer of human behavior. What's the difference? The difference is awareness.

Over time, I came to see people as individuals, as opposed to nameless faces in a crowd. I observe people performing to their potential. I see students achieving amazing successes in their chosen fields of endeavor. I see fathers and mothers modeling life choices and values for their children to emulate. I see businessmen and businesswomen sharing expertise in service to their communities.

With heightened awareness comes the realization that human endeavors do not always reap the desired results. Individuals who engage in destructive behaviors circumvent not only their own capabilities, but also deny those in their sphere of existence the opportunity to grow and excel.

Humans are complex, multifaceted beings. We have all known people who are supremely confident and capable in their occupations, but at the same time they seem to struggle to maintain healthy and positive relationships in their personal lives. Some people engage in a constant battle to attain specific financial goals, while putting their health at risk in the process. Others find it difficult to discern true purpose in their lives due to an absence of a spiritual component.

Mental health issues certainly play an important part in life choices as well.

How is it we can excel in one area of our life and struggle in another? Why is it we let opportunities pass us by, then look back years later and wonder why we never got a break? If we are brave enough to dream, why can't we honor that little voice inside of us and try? Why don't we do the simple things in life that, clearly, will keep us healthy?

In my early twenties, I was still just a people watcher. My mother and I were watching a television show together one day, and we witnessed yet another life lived as a train wreck waiting to happen. I commented that I thought people give themselves way too much credit. Look at the mess these folks were making of their lives.

My mother thought otherwise. "Actually, I don't think people give themselves enough credit. They act out of control at times, making bad decisions and then giving up on themselves at the earliest disappointment. I believe they don't realize how truly capable they are. They don't give themselves enough credit.

It was quite a few years before I came to understand my mother was right. It is now my goal to help people realize what I finally came to recognize. We are all more capable than we know. We can live dynamic, productive lives. We can move others to build on the momentum we create each time we confront our challenges. I visualize this momentum expanding to worldwide proportions. I call it Life Momentum.

The objectives outlined in *Your Life Is Your Business* are within your reach. By applying a combination of scientific knowledge, common sense, proven business practices, and reason in your daily life, you will create the momentum in your life that will provide the balance and the motivation to reach your goals.

Keep these terms uppermost in your mind as you learn more about Life Momentum.

Awareness: The concept and importance of paying attention

Mindfulness: The benefits of an alert, in the moment, existence

Mental Power: Understanding the brain is a powerful machine

Honesty, Trust, Awareness, Growth: The connectedness of these qualities

Clarity: Seeing things as they are; having an honest view of yourself

Momentum: The principle of the energy you generate with an action plan

The Gap: The space between where we are and where we want to be

Tools: Methods and strategies to set energy in motion to gain momentum

A careful reading of *Your Life Is Your Business* will enable you to:

- Understand the concept and importance of awareness
- Discover the joy of living a mindful, in the moment, existence
- Reach an appropriate and practical understanding of the power of the mind

- Understand the connections between honesty, trust, awareness, and growth
- Know and use the tools that will help you create and maintain momentum
- Utilize the concept of clarity to get yourself on track and stay on track

Let me introduce you to a formula I use in my personal life, as well as in my professional life. I call it **Good—Better—Best**. By reading *Your Life Is Your Business*, you will get an excellent picture of how you can best pattern and conduct your life so that you are in charge. This is a *good* beginning to understanding the importance of creating the momentum in your life that will help you achieve your goals.

You may want to dig deeper to learn more about this material. For that purpose, related information, exercises, reflections, and Internet links are available at the Momentum Builders, Inc. website. This additional information will give you even more value and a *better* experience by enhancing your understanding of the principles put forward in this book.

Your *best* results will be realized by working the Online Life Momentum Action Plan Workbook or the printable Life Momentum Action Plan Workbook. Instructions for retrieving this information can be found in the Wrap Up Section at the end of *Your Life Is Your Business*.

Working with either one of these programs will offer you the opportunity of making your life what you want it to be. You will establish and work your Action Plan by devoting a small amount of time each day to creating momentum and establishing balance in your life.

Your Life Is Your Business

LESSONS IN BUILDING A LIFE OF MOMENTUM:

IT IS NEVER TOO late, nor too early, to discover your mission. The most difficult step is often the first one: getting started. Life Momentum can help you get over that hurdle. The challenges you will face will be rigorous. You will learn how to recognize and acknowledge the presence of an inner voice that urges you to press on. You can do more; you can become a better you. You will be guided to the place where your vision and inner voice are leading you. There is no doubt you can achieve more than you have to date, and there is no doubt we can help you get there and thrive there.

Use *Your Life Is Your Business* as a handy guide to take you from where you are today to where you want to be. You will gain the knowledge and acquire the tools to build and maintain momentum. This book begins by challenging you to identify your purpose, your vision, and your personal values. The pages that follow focus on the tools you will need for success and a quick review of the value of awareness. The body of the book guides you through a review of each of the pieces in your life and the necessary steps to improve in each area.

The power and functions of your mind are explained throughout. You will be challenged, supported, and ushered to a better place in each aspect of life as you go through the process of creating your personal action plan. Know what actions you should take, and then take action before someone else does it for you. If you want to save the world, or improve it, build a better you with Life Momentum.

In order to succeed, we must first believe that we can.

~Nikos Kazantzakis, Greek Philosopher

Momentum Builders Inc.©

Our Premise:

People are more capable than they realize.

Our Mission:

To help you move from where you are to where you want to be.

The Life Momentum Vision:

Millions of people work the Life Momentum program,

improving their lives and the lives around them.

The world gains momentum.

Mission + Vision x Action = **Life Momentum**

Chapter One

Introduction to Life Momentum

Coming out of your comfort zone is tough in the beginning, chaotic in the middle, and awesome in the end because in the end, it shows you a whole new world! Make an attempt.

~Manoj Aror

YOUR LIFE IS YOUR Business was developed to introduce a new way of thinking. It is a way that requires you to take charge of your life. It is a way by which you welcome opportunities and challenges. It is a way in which you will see structure and balance as necessary foundations for a successful and fulfilled life.

The fact that you have opened this book and are reading these words indicates you are intrigued by the notion of imagining your life as a business. In business, if you don't improve and grow, your business becomes stagnant. So it is in life.

Look at these images of the man operating a flywheel. Getting started on any project takes strength and will. Change is

hard, but change can also be exhilarating. Excitement generates energy; energy generates momentum.

Take a deep breath. Develop a plan. Don't waste time and
energy on negatives. Visualize what you want your future to
be, then concentrate on that reality and the steps it takes to
get there. Start building your momentum. Enthusiasm will
ultimately replace anxiety.

Bridging the Gap

MY REPUTATION AS A strategic planner is built on helping individuals to stay proactive in order to bridge the gap of where they are to where they want to be. Each time you stretch your goals and re-create your vision, you create a gap. You will be armed with information and techniques for bridging that gap and getting to where you want to be.

If you come away with nothing else from reading *Your Life Is Your Business,* remember how important it is to be vigilant; that idea should resonate with you throughout your lifetime. It is the reason that the awareness factor is stressed over and over again.

Early detection (awareness) of any lapse of interest or self-motivation on your part is your cue to return to the basics. Read your mission and vision statements. Remind yourself what you did early in the process to create and build your momentum. Revisit the various tools that got you started:

Where I am today/Where I want to be

Issues and Ideas Dump

Honesty and Awareness

Decision-making

Affirmations

The Reticular Activating System

They got you where you are and they will help you to bridge the gap and get you to where you want to be. You have the desire. You have the ability. You have access to the knowledge.

Build the structure that will support your mission and vision to get you from where you are to where you want to be.

The Action Plan Introduction

A working definition of: The Action Plan

YOUR ACTION PLAN IS your daily checkup, planning, and motivational tool. It provides a view into your future. Most of your life's details can reside on the Action Plan. Fifteen minutes a day with your Action Plan will keep your life in order and moving in a positive direction.

> *When it is obvious that the goals cannot be reached, don't adjust the goals, adjust the action steps*
>
> ~Confucius

Working the Action Plan

THE FRAMEWORK OF THE Action Plan is designed to encourage self-awareness. The Action Plan provides a method of assessing and analyzing progress in ten specific areas of your life.

These aspects are outlined in the Life Momentum Wheel as integral parts of the whole. Refer to the back of the book for information on downloading the online Action Plan Workbook. A printed version of the Action Plan Workbook is located in the appendix of *Your Life is Your Business*.

To retrieve an online Action Plan or a printable copy of the Action Plan Workbook, visit:

momentumbuildersinc.com/registernow

Enter Serial number 24682468A.

As you navigate the workbook, you will be prompted to place updates on your Action Plan. You are creating a living document to guide you on a timely basis while keeping a focus on your daily and long-range goals. Literally every priority of your life will be managed and advanced on the Action Plan.

The Action Plan will help you realize that all of the identified pieces in your life are connected. A few minutes each day spent on input and assessment will keep you on track, energized, and ready for the next opportunity or challenge.

This is not an afternoon project. This is a lifelong project. In working the Action Plan, you will come to realize the primary motivating factor for human beings is the sense of achievement that comes from consistent progress and steady improvement. These factors are vital to the creation of even more energy, excitement, and momentum to stay on course.

Once you grasp this concept, you will be empowered to take charge of your life, to live your mission, to pursue your vision, and to be the best "YOU" you can be. Let's begin this journey together. Let's start right now!

The Brain on an Action Plan

~Amy Guy

SIMON SINEK IS A leadership guru, professor at Columbia University, and founder of Sinek Partners. Sinek advances the idea that behavior is grounded in the tenets of biology, rather than the more commonly held belief that behavior is grounded in psychology.

In this context, Sinek describes the brain in this way: The neocortex corresponds with the "what" level and is responsible for all rational and analytical thought and language. The middle two sections make up our limbic brains. The limbic brains are responsible for feelings such as trust and loyalty. Sinek points out that the limbic brains are also responsible for all human behavior, all decision-making, but that it has no capacity for language.

Another way to describe this relationship of the brain and behavior is to address the issues of the "what" and the "why" of our actions. For instance, communication from the outside in allows us to understand facts and figures and other complicated information. The "what" does not drive personal behavior. On the other hand, when we communicate from the inside out (the why), we are talking directly to the part of the brain that does control behavior.

Sinek provides us with this example. You may have all the facts and details to form a decision, but something about the process just doesn't "feel" right. We have all experienced that gut reaction, an inner feeling that is not based on facts. This is happening in your limbic brain, the part of the brain that controls decision-making and not language.

The point of all this is to help you reach an awareness and an understanding of yourself. It should be important to you to want to know what inspires and motivates you in all areas of your life. If you never really understand the why of your dreams and aspirations, how can you ever hope to make those dreams come true?

Real Life Examples of the Action Plan

~Amy Guy

RECENTLY, WHILE ATTENDING A church service, I found myself sitting beside a former student of CEO (Creating Entrepreneurial Opportunities) class. Later, as we walked out of church together, I took the opportunity to ask how he was doing. He gave a cheerless shrug of his shoulders and then answered, "Okay, I guess." He then admitted that he was struggling to get a schedule formulated, and he wasn't comfortable in his new dorm room. He was pretty vague with all of his comments and complaints. What wasn't vague was the sense that this young man needed a refresher course. He reported that he hadn't been lifting or working out at all. His physical health was not where it should be. I told him it sounded as though he'd lost his momentum, and all aspects of his life were suffering as a result. He definitely agreed that was the case.

While this young man was in CEO class, he learned how to develop and work an Action Plan. When I asked him if he was still working his plan, his response was a lackluster, "Well, kind of." *Kind of* really never cuts it. We then talked about how hard it is to go from being a big fish in a small pond to a small fish in a big pond. This young man had some big changes happening in his life, but he didn't need to feel confused and defeated. I encouraged him to reach back into his bag of tricks (his Action Plan) to meet these challenges. He just needed to remind himself how capable he once was, and that he will be successful again.

Lives are not static. Each of our lives is always changing. Normally, change comes in small, easily managed doses. Sometimes changes are life altering and require a well-thought-out response. An Action Plan is a life plan—and, yes, one size fits all events. That's the beauty of the Action Plan. If you work it, it will work for you.

Incremental Improvements

HOW DO YOU GET to the top of a mountain? Take one step at a time.

Success in life comes in stages. Where you are now is your *starting point.* Where you want to be is your *vision.* How you get there is by living your mission. Most of life's successes come from doing the right things every day while being aware of long-term goals.

Progress may come in small increments at first. This is natural when adapting to a new way of looking at your life. This is the purpose of the Action Plan, and it's why it is so important for developing and implementing your daily activities. The process of mapping your progress will help you stay on track. Seeing advancements and improvements in your life will empower you to stay true to your goals and dreams. Change may seem small, but larger successes are supported by the actions you take on a daily basis.

If you are not growing, you are falling behind. The number one motivating factor for most people is seeing how their efforts are making a difference and improving their lives. That is when it's okay to give yourself a pat on the back for the commitment you are making to challenge yourself and your willingness to change when necessary.

How do you eat an elephant? Take one bite at a time!

How do you build momentum? Work your Action Plan!

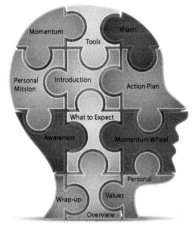

Tools: Exercises and Building Skills

Working definition of Tools:

THE MOMENTUM BUILDING TOOLS refer to methods to help you to be proactive in your mission, move past obstacles as they arise, and bring clarity in understanding and defining your vision.

Think of these tactics as tools for your life. I, and people I work with, have come to appreciate the important role all of these strategic steps play in fostering positive outcomes in whatever process I'm engaged in. The simplicity of these tools is so natural and authentic that you might wonder why you haven't discovered them sooner. For our purposes, let's call them the five tools of momentum building.

Where I am today/Where I want to be

Issues and Ideas Dump

Honesty and Awareness

Decision-making

Affirmations

Reticular Activating System

We become what we behold.
We shape our tools, and thereafter our tools shape us.

~Marshall McLuhan, Canadian Educator

Where I am Today/Where I want to be

YOU CAN'T PLAN A trip if you don't know where you want to go. If you don't know where you are now, you can't decide how far you have to travel to get to where you want to go. To address this situation, you will utilize the first of the tools offered in this book. It is the *Where I am/Where I want to be* tool.

Using the Action Plan, estimate your present level of success with regard to each of your life pieces. As the *Where I am* tool becomes second nature, you will find it to be a valuable asset throughout your life. The more you are aware of the facts of your present situation, the more comfortable you will become in trusting your own gut feelings when making important decisions. Whenever you feel stuck or in a rut, this exercise can get you up and running. It will help you identify the initiatives needed to get you to where you want to be.

Personal awareness is the key to making this tool function in the manner intended. At each step, an honest assessment of where you are now is essential. Here is an example of how to use this tool: Identify in detail all that you know about the current status of a challenge or an opportunity facing you. Momentum Builders refers to this stage as *Where I am*. Now you want to look ahead and determine where you wish to see yourself. This is called *Where I want to be*.

Take a full accounting of both where you are and where you want to be; then decide what actions are needed to move you in the right direction. You will place these steps on your Action Plan. Each step will have a clear description of the action, a description of what the action will entail, and a specific date for its completion. The act of logging the various steps is, itself, a time-saver. As you follow each step to conclusion, you'll see the anxiety factor disappear. Each time you follow this blueprint, you'll become aware that you are moving in a positive direction, you are becoming more confident in trusting yourself and your decisions, and your energy level is higher. You are gaining momentum.

WHERE I   WHERE I
AM TODAY   WANT TO BE

Issues and Ideas Dump

"I HAVE A MILLION things to do today. I have so much on my mind I don't know where to start!" Sound familiar? The statement is, of course, an exaggeration. The concern, however, is not. We have all been in this boat at one time or another. There is so much to do and so little time in which to do it. But wait. Obviously, fretting over something is not really doing anything about it. Worry only makes problems loom larger and appear worse than they are.

This is where you grab the next tool: *Issues and Ideas Dump*.

Imagine an analogy in which the myriad projects crowding your mind are like marbles in your head. As you become frustrated and discouraged, mental pressure builds and the marbles begin bouncing around like crazy. It seems as though there are hundreds. It is impossible to even attempt to keep track of the number of marbles. In real life, with issues whirling and spinning in your mind, a similar response will cause you to feel overwhelmed and incapable of tackling the issues before you. But the good news is, the remedy to this situation is completely within your control.

The first step is to empty your mind of the many issues that are bogging you down by writing each one on a checklist. Review the list and select one or two of the easiest projects to accomplish. Refer to your Action Plan and place the accomplished items in the completed section. You will feel an immediate sense of accomplishment. In fact, your brain will give you a shot of dopamine as a reward. A boost of do-pamine gets you on your way to building momentum. In this positive frame of mind, you will review the rest of the items on your Action Plan with less angst and more enthusiasm. Do not carry more than one or two action items in your head at any one time. Dump the rest on your Action Plan. You will establish a pattern of prioritizing, which will help you in all areas of your life. The key is to employ the *Issues and Ideas Dump* on a regular basis and add to your momentum build-ing tools.

ISSUES AND IDEAS

Honesty

FEW PERSONAL TRAITS ARE as powerful as honesty. Complete honesty empowers. The absence of honesty undermines progress. In the words of Sigmund Freud, "Being entirely honest with oneself is a good exercise."

Honesty is where trust of self and others resides. If you are not honest with yourself, can you trust yourself? If you cannot trust yourself, will you trust others? Lack of honesty undermines self-confidence. Your progress in momentum-building relies heavily on an honest evaluation of yourself. Think of this evaluation process as a way of taking a personal inventory of your strengths, your weaknesses, your fears, your hopes, your biases, and any other concerns or traits that make up who you are. This is not an easy task. Though it is not always easy to look in the mirror under the harsh light of reality, it is the first big step on the journey that is the rest of your life.

There is liberation in truth and honesty. Though we strive to be the best we can be, a dose of realism is a necessary component of this process. If, or when, you fall short in some way, make amends for that slip and get back on track right away. Do not dwell on the missteps. Learn from them and let the momentum roll on.

When in doubt tell the truth. It will confound your enemies and as-tound your friends.

~Mark Twain

HONESTY

Decision-making

WHAT IS YOUR DECISION-MAKING process? Are you thorough in discerning the various aspects involved in the decision? Do you make decisions in a timely fashion? Do you tend to procrastinate and make partial decisions while leaving the issue as a whole unresolved?

Each of us makes a variety of decisions on a daily basis, evenly hourly for that matter. Obviously, some decisions carry more weight than others and, thus, are more important than others. We've already introduced two tools that will help you in decision-making: the *Where I am/Where I want to be* tool and the personal Honesty tool. Utilizing these tools will provide you with a starting point for your decision-making action.

Both the *Where I am/Where I want to be* tool and the *Honesty* tool require you to gather all facts and information pertinent to the decision at hand. With facts on your side, decisions will be based on reason first. At this point, you will wisely assess the proposed decision by taking your instincts and gut feeling into consideration. Combining these aspects will give you a better chance at making the right decision.

Here is an example of a real-life decision-making process. Assume you have good information on an important issue. There are five options available to you. This is where you will have to trust your intuition or gut feeling. Take the leap and make the decision. Waiting and procrastinating will not make it easier. In this scenario, the first decision turns out to be the wrong one. Again, do not put off dealing with the decision. Ask yourself what you learned from pursuing this decision that made it the wrong decision. Now you have new information with which to make a new decision. One of the five options is now off the table. The new information you gleaned may help you discard another two of the original options. Your chances of success are significantly better than the first time around. Continue this process until you arrive at the right option. Individuals and companies as a whole can suffer serious reversals if they freeze and don't take a stance and make a decision. Making timely and fact-based decisions helps build and maintain your MOMENTUM.

DECISION MAKING

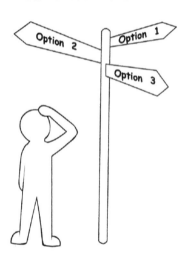

Affirmations

AN AFFIRMATION IS AN emotional support and a type of encouragement. Affirmations provide a simple but effective tool, easily incorporated into your daily life.

An affirmation, simply stated, is YOU making a declarative statement ABOUT YOU that you want to program your mind to believe. Understanding that the mind believes what we tell it teaches us that the more we compose and deliver credible affirmations, the more likely the desired outcome will prevail. This is not wishful thinking. We each have the ability to create new pathways in the brain. To begin to understand the power an individual has over the biology of the brain you have only to realize that you would have to learn something new every second for 3 million years to begin to challenge its capacity. Famed, neurosurgeon, Dr. Ben Carson, regularly presents these startling facts as he lectures around the country, encouraging people to concentrate more on what they can do than what they can not do.

Affirmations are effective tools in creating these new pathways. An affirmation is a conscious thought that we place purposefully into our mind's awareness to help us train the brain to believe it is the truth. The unconscious mind also has great influence on our thoughts and feelings. If your experience with affirmations has been unhelpful in the past, you will find it useful to identify the beliefs you hold that oppose the affirmations. You might begin by making a list of negative qualities you identify in yourself. Often these may have come by way of parents, peers, siblings or co-workers. Do not judge the accuracy of these impressions. Do not be defensive. Simply make a list of the flaws. Once you have your list, write an affirmation to counteract each of the negative affirmations you currently hold.

Now you are ready to speak the affirmation out loud to yourself or begin to write it in a daily journal. The act of writing the affirmation helps reinforce it in a different way than simply stating it. You may notice the way you write your affirmation will change over time.

An effective way to incorporate the affirmation into your life (make it yours), is to anchor what you are saying into your breathing patterns. Such as, breathe in and repeat, "I am ..." breathe out and say, "a marathon runner." The goal is to move the affirmation from being a declarative sentence about ourselves to something we embody in our very nature. Envision it first as being like leaves on a tree, eventually being a part of the root system of that tree. It becomes who you are and will be rooted in your very being.

The purpose of this exercise is to help you reach an awareness and an understanding of yourself. It should be important to you to want to know what inspires and motivates you in all areas of your life. If you never really understand the *why* of your dreams and aspirations, how can you ever hope to make those dreams come true?

To understand exactly how this process works, that of programming your unconscious mind with affirmations of positivity, read the following article which describes the brain's Reticular Activating System.

AFFIRMATION

The Reticular Activating System

YOUR BRAIN'S RETICULAR ACTIVATING System plays a vital part in your ability to achieve your target goals.

Imagine the RAS as a "customizable filter". Because our minds are bombarded with stimuli from our environment, the miraculous machine that is our brain is able to filter, adapt, and react to particular stimuli. Even more amazing is the fact that individuals can input information that will affect this filter. This is where the importance of *affirmations* comes into play. The act of regularly speaking desirable and specific statements over a substantial period of time will actually "mold" the filter (RAS) to this new mindset. The new convictions and new thoughts making their way into your subconscious will provide access to a wealth of opportunities as you capitalize on this heightened awareness.

Your reticular activating system is like a filter between your conscious mind and your subconscious mind. It takes instructions from your conscious mind and passes them on to your subconscious. For example, the instruction might be, "Listen out for anyone saying my name."

There are some interesting points about your RAS that make it an essential tool for achieving goals.

First, you can deliberately **program** the reticular activating system by choosing the exact messages you send from your conscious mind. For example, you can **set goals**, or say **affirmations**, or **visualize your goals**. We can achieve any realistic goal if we keep on thinking of that goal and stop thinking any negative thoughts about it. Of course, if we keep thinking that we cannot achieve a goal, our subconscious will help us NOT achieve it.

Second, your reticular activating system cannot distinguish between "real events" and "synthetic" reality. In other words, it tends to believe whatever message you give it. Imagine that you're going to be giving a speech. You can practice giving that speech by visualizing it in your mind. This "pretend" practice should improve your ability to give the speech.

What we need to do is to create a very specific picture of our goal in our conscious mind. The RAS will then pass this on to our subconscious, which will then help us achieve the goal. It does this by bringing to our attention all the relevant information that might otherwise have remained as "background noise".

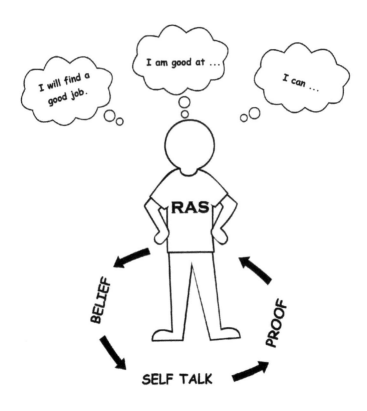

Chapter Two

Personal Mission Statement Overview

Working definition of Personal Mission Statement:

> "A mission statement is not something you write overnight ... But fundamentally, your mission statement becomes your constitution, the solid expression of your vision and values. It becomes the criterion by which you measure everything else in your life."

> ~Stephen Richard Covey, author, educator

Personal Mission Statement Introduction

Your purpose, the reason you exist

"why do i need to take the time to write a mission statement?" "How does this apply to me?"

I suggest a well-thought-out mission statement is something we could all benefit from. Understanding and defining a mission statement is the very first step in gaining control over your life and achieving your goals and dreams. Your mission statement, your purpose, or the phrase, "my WHY," once articulated, will be an invaluable reference and guide for the rest of your life.

Most successful companies have a mission statement, a defined purpose, which they need in order to survive and prosper in the competitive world marketplace. Why are we, as individuals, any different? Contemplate for a minute how you think companies become great, unique, driven, and successful? They start with an idea, just like every other company, entrepreneur, and inventor. The successful companies took up their idea and they lived it, they focused on it each and every day. It became part of who they are and they own it; it is their reason for existing. These companies say no to opportunities that aren't in alignment with their purpose. They say yes" to the opportunities that fit their purpose. The companies armed with a defined purpose can navigate the obstacles and hard times along the way because they have a guiding light. That guiding light is their *mission statement*.

I believe this same principle applies to individuals. In fact, I've seen it over and over again. My clients, armed with a stated mission, are more committed, have better peace of mind, and consistently stay on task. Therefore, they become more accomplished. These individuals say yes to the things they know will serve them well in life, and they say no to those things that are going to take them off task.

The mission statement is clear, consistent, and dependable; it is a declaration to support all future plans. Think of your mission statement as your home base. It is the starting point from which you will make decisions regarding the path to fulfilling your dreams and goals. When life becomes uncertain or confusing, you know you can return to your home base for safety and clarity and the opportunity to recharge before you continue on your mission.

It is not easy to fully understand and come to terms with establishing your mission statement. It takes work on your part. It will take time and a heightened awareness of where you are in your life. Complete honesty throughout this process is imperative. The more raw, organic, and truthful you can be with yourself, the more you will benefit from the process. There is light at the end of the tunnel!

Think of this as a golden opportunity to begin to realize that your dreams and goals are attainable. I encourage you to do your best at this stage. It is understandable, and acceptable, that you may find yourself refining and clarifying your mission statement. If you cannot clearly state your purpose, however, your first task is to discover your purpose. The search will be well worth the struggle.

Here are some questions you can ask yourself to help develop your mission statement:

What motivates me?

What deeply interests me?

In what do I strongly believe?

What excites me?

What matters to me?

What inspires me?

Keep your vision in mind as you develop your mission statement. The mission and vision state statements must fit together.

The Brain on a Mission

~Amy Guy

HOW WOULD YOU ANSWER the question, "What is your mission in life?" If you happen to be a teenager, you might answer that you strive to get good grades in school. Perhaps you answer that you hope to achieve success in a particular sport or artistic endeavor. These are typical and worthwhile goals. Achievements are important steps in building momentum in your life. Each stage reached provides satisfaction and gratification. However, at some point, you realize that life is about more than specific short-term goals that provide immediate satisfaction.

A mission in life is that which fully prepares you to experience life. Finding your mission is crucial to ongoing health, happiness, and well-being. Mission gives us energy and is what gets us out of bed each morning. Living with a mission takes PRACTICE. This is true. By now we have learned that anything worthwhile takes practice to make it an integral part of our lives. In the everyday hustle and bustle of life, it is easy to set our actions to autopilot. This is not conducive to developing and nurturing your momentum. Mission helps us focus on how we want to live our lives. We call this living mindfully.

Pay attention and live with intention. Reading and focusing on your purpose in life will help program your mind and body to live in the moment, to live mindfully.

Say your mission as an affirmation statement each morning and evening. It may surprise you to see how quickly you adopt this new awareness. You will begin to think bigger and more positively. Our mission is to look forward always, focusing our mind and energy on how we want to live our lives.

Mission Statements of Successful and Famous People

Outstanding people have one thing in common: An absolute sense of mission.

~Zig Ziglar, author and motivational speaker

Denise Morrison, CEO of Campbell Soup Company: "To serve as a leader, live a balanced life, and apply ethical principles to make a significant difference."

Dr. Joseph Hartmann, Cardiologist: "Live long, live well."

Oprah Winfrey: "To be a teacher and to be known for inspiring my students to be more than they thought they could be."

Sir Richard Branson: "To have fun in my journey through life and learn from my mistakes. I find enjoyment in my personal life through traveling and finding new places to explore. I find opportunities to use my natural talents and gifts such as art, being a good friend, a creative thinker to help others around me."

Walt Disney: "I dream, I test my dreams against my beliefs, I dare to take risks and I execute my vision to make those dreams come true."

Joel Manby, CEO of Herschend Family Entertainment: "I define personal success as being consistent to my own personal mission statement: to love God and love others."

Amanda Steinberg, founder of DailyWorth.com: "To use my gifts of intelligence, charisma, and serial optimism to cultivate the self-worth and net-worth of women around the world."

Chapter Three

Personal Vision Overview

Working definition of Vision Statement:

YOUR FUTURE, WRITTEN IN present tense with imagination, creativity, inspiration, and with your mission statement in mind. Your mission statement and vision statement must be in line with one another. The more you know yourself, the easier it will be to write your vision statement.

Vision Introduction:

DREAMS, ASPIRATIONS, AND GOALS MAKE UP YOUR VISION

"PAIN PUSHES ... UNTIL vision pulls." This is a powerful statement. It really hits home when you realize we are talking about two strong motivators. Take a moment to remember the last time you had pain in your life. Maybe you are in pain right now. I am referring to pain that comes from frustration. Perhaps bad decisions led to bad outcomes. Perhaps you didn't make a decision at all, and you were left to the whim and mercy of others to steer the course for you.

Let's take a closer look at pain as a motivator. Pain pushes. We normally don't get to choose what kind of pain we suffer, or its severity, or even how long we suffer from the pain. It does get us moving and prompts us to take action, but in what direction? What did your pain feel like? Why did the pain occur? In what direction did the pain push you? What did you do about the pain? What control did you really have over the pain once it began?

Now let's look at vision as a motivator. Vision pulls. By definition, vision is the direction in which we want to go. Our vision tells us when and how far we want to go and how much time and emotional output we are willing to expend. We have clarity of and control over our vision. Think of a time when you were responsible for planning an important group activity. You attended to every detail, and the results were spectacular. It exceeded your initial hopes and the vision you had for its outcome. How did you feel about the planning aspect of the project? Was it fun or was it laborious? How did it make you feel to be able to accomplish your goal? How did it feel to visualize a positive outcome and then pursue that project to its successful outcome? Did you interact with others to accomplish your goal? How was that experience? Were others willing to help? Did the personal energy you drew on as head of this project have the effect of energizing your fellow workers? Did you find it a positive reaction that those helping were able to accept your vision, thus making it a smoother and more pleasant process for all involved?

When a painful situation pushes you in one way or another, you are forced to react. You may not have the luxury of choosing that reaction. When you are in charge, you are able to let your vision pull you in a direction of your choosing. In which realm would you rather participate: pain or vision? Do you see the difference between pain pushing and vision pulling?

One of the most important aspects about being human is having the ability to dream, hope, set personal goals, reach them, exceed them, and have new goals already in place.

The mission statement discussed in the previous lesson defines your purpose and your home base. The subject of this lesson, your *vision statement*, is made up of your dreams and aspirations. It marks out the direction you choose to take, with your home base in mind. Having a clear vision is an important step in attaining your dreams and goals. It is important to write your vision statement with emotion, color, and feeling. It should be exciting and motivating to you every time you read it. In truth, your vision statement can be both exciting and frightening. You will experience a heightened level of energy. This sense of fear or anxiety is natural and accompanies the commitment to a properly crafted vision statement. Why? Because your vision statement challenges you to commit to dreams and goals you don't currently know how to achieve.

Building life momentum is exciting and challenging. Committing to your own vision, writing it down, and aspiring to move toward it each and every day will, and should, draw you outside of your comfort zone. When you commit to the process, the energy and the excitement that will result are exactly the energy you'll need to succeed. Lou Tice, founder of the Pacific Institute, does a wonderful job of explaining this incredible capacity of man. This ability that exists in our minds—when properly directed—to get us what we want is one of the strongest arguments for the Life Momentum premise: We are all capable of success. The two steps of writing your mission and vision statements will have made a substantial contribution to the overall day-to-day momentum you build and help you tap into this little-understood ability.

Imagine going to bed every night excited to get up the next day, full of purpose and energy, in hot pursuit of your dreams and aspirations. It will happen when you begin living your mission and vision statements and begin to enjoy the progress you are making. You will be excited for morning to come so you can get back to your life's work. You will put everything you have, and even power you may not yet know you possess, into it because you know that what you are doing matters.

This is Life Momentum.

The Brain on a Vision

~Amy Guy

DID YOU KNOW THAT even before events happen, the brain has already made a prediction about what is most likely to happen? It sets in motion the perception, behaviors, emotions, physiological responses, and interpersonal ways of relating that best fit with its prediction.

Amazing as this sounds, psychiatrist Dr. Regina Pally states that studies in the field of neuroscience tell us "we learn from the past what to predict for the future and then live the future we expect."

Perhaps NBA superstar Michael Jordan put it more succinctly: "You have to expect things of yourself before you can do them."

Continuing to refer to studies in the field of neuroscience, it is much easier to achieve something if you can visualize yourself already achieving it. As we struggle over creating our mission and vision statements, we are forced to focus on our desired future and to consolidate that future in our mind. Even without being consciously aware, our brain begins to set in motion that which is needed to make this outcome possible.

There are activities to promote this reaction. Here are two examples.

Pretend it is five years from now and you are living in your ideal future. Write several diary entries pertaining to that future. Visualize this scene: you are attending a talk as part of a large audience. Everyone in the audience is deeply touched and inspired by the speaker. The speaker is you, fifteen years from now. Ideas move from the impossible to the improbable, from the improbable to the possible, then, finally, the possible to the actionable. In other words, the more we talk about our vision, the more we envision it actually happening, and the greater the chance it becomes possible.

Helpful Examples of Visions

My company offers travel into outer space, and my creativity inspires and challenges millions to be more.

My foundation builds schools in Africa, where there are none, to help spread my message to young girls.

I have a nationally syndicated radio show that promotes and teaches financial literacy to millions so they can change their lives and their children's lives.

Millions of people follow the Life Momentum program, improving their lives and the lives of others. I have published books that challenge, encourage, and help people discover their personal mission.

I am strong, healthy, and fit. I am pain free, able to work creatively and joyfully in my role of hands-on mom, relaxed, and content knowing I am financially secure and debt free.

I joyfully do work which profits both my pocket and my soul. I am energized traveling to amazing places, spending time with wonderful and diverse people, sharing knowledge, and expanding my horizons.

I have a fulfilling relationship with my adult children, I am an active walker with many friends along the way, and I am writing another book, which empowers me and benefits my readers.

I am a cardiologist and a loving active parent. I am trusted and enjoy helping others with all things medical.

Create Your Personal Vision Statement:

TO BEGIN, WRITE YOUR vision statement in the present tense (as if it is happening now). It should be personal, with emotion and expressive. A vision statement is a description of how you see your future. Your ideal future can be described as your "stretch goal", indicating a goal far from your present situation. There is no way you will know every step it will take to move toward this ideal future. The idea of the "stretch goal" is to continue the challenges you set for yourself, not putting limits on what your ideal future might be.

As you gather momentum, your ideal future may change, and you may find yourself inspired to push even harder toward your immediate goals. Your stretch goal may change. What once you thought impossible may soon seem attainable. Your goal is to push hard toward a difficult but reasonable and reachable endgame. (Having a vision to be six feet tall would be considered unreasonable if you are presently a 5' 8" adult.)

To begin, review the questions below. Identify a key word or phrase from each answer. This will help you develop your vision statement.

- What was your life like five years ago?
- What are your strengths and abilities?
- What do you do best and enjoy doing?
- What are your favorite activities?
- What are you most passionate about?
- When do you go to bed feeling excited about getting up the next day?
- What are three things you would like to do every day?
- When do you feel best about yourself and your life?
- What pieces of your life are most important to you?
- What pieces of your life do you want never to deal with again?
- Do you treat yourself and others well on a consistent basis?
- When do you have the most energy and the best attitude?
- When is your energy low and your attitude the worst?
- Name one or two things you want to be good or excellent at doing?
- What type of people do you enjoy being around and why?
- What do you like to daydream about?

After you have written down all of your answers, look for words or phrases from each answer that can help you start your vision statement. I encourage you to get something written down.

You can refine your vision statement as you go through the program. Your mission statement will change little, if at all.

Your vision statement will change as you accomplish goals. Remember the "stretch goal" progression.

As you garner new facts and new ideas, your course of action may veer in a new direction. It is crucial to your success to keep a vision in mind that challenges and excites you while at the same time is in harmony with, and supported by, your mission statement.

Vision without action is merely a dream. Action without vision just passes the time. Vision with action can change the world.

~Joel A. Barker, Futurist, Author, Lecturer

Chapter Four

Personal Values Statement Overview

Personal Values Introduction

The Brain on Personal Values

Helpful Examples of Personal Values

Personal Values Statement Overview

Working definition of Personal Values:

     PERSONAL VALUES ARE THE core beliefs, standards, and ethics we hold regarding life, its purpose, and our own purpose. As children, we adopt the personal values reflected by those closest to us. Maturity brings a period of discernment. We begin to accept or reject values, taking stock of ourselves, pinpointing our own values, and making them a part of our lives. This guide will walk you through the process as you embrace and nurture your most deeply held personal values, which will create a solid foundation for you to ground your choices and decisions in positive motives and commitment to your beliefs.

Personal Values Introduction:

THE BELIEFS THAT GUIDE YOUR LIFE

VISUALIZE A PERSON WHO possesses a positive, confident, self-assured demeanor. Now imagine a person filled with self-doubt, distrust of others, and difficulty navigating either his work or social environment. A variety of factors may account for this stark difference. One might be that the first individual possesses a strong values system. The second individual appears to have little direction in his or her life and seems to have a suspicious nature. People's lives are shaped by the values they espouse. Those who hold honesty as a stated value are not only honest with others, but with themselves as well. A person who is mistrustful of others often has issues with his or her own honesty. Those of us unable to look in the mirror and see the person as the world views us may be lacking in honesty.

Honesty and integrity go hand in hand. Both in business and personal relationships, integrity is a valuable asset. To know that a man's word is his bond is to know he is upright, truthful, and reliable. These are solid values that will guide you as you navigate your life's journey. It is important for each of us to make an accounting of exactly what values we choose to live by. Many of us will be in agreement on most. Some will place certain values on a higher plane than others.

The critical concern is that we name our values, take full account of what each really means to us, and go about making them a central part of who we are.

Writing your personal values statement, then committing to align your actions with it, will provide you with an important tool to guide you and remind you who you are and what is important to you when making decisions, taking actions, and dealing with stress and pressure.

As I work with companies in my consulting capacity, I take stock of what I see as being the company's culture and its values. This is the part of a company you cannot capture in a snapshot, yet it is a part that is very real and vitally important to a company's success. How do employees at all levels work with each other? How does the staff treat company property? How are customers treated and cared for? Like its mission and vision statements, a company's stated culture, their values system, provides a guide to stay on track, a reminder that everyone in the organization promised to honor his or her commitment to those values.

In the competitive world of business, it makes sense that a company with a strong, value-based culture will be more successful than one not living up to their stated values. A blanket statement of culture we use is, "Establish and maintain relationships and conditions suitable for personal and corporate growth." When I do an opening interview with clients, I ask them what is important to them, what they value most in their lives, and how they rate themselves on a scale of 1–10. One of the first clients I ever worked with said he valued, among other things, being a great father to his three children. When I asked him to rate himself on some key aspects of his life, he rated himself in this way.

He gave himself a 5 for being a thoughtful, caring husband; 2 as a provider of his family; 3 for his honesty; 2 as a role model for his children. Sadly, as I was asking another question, he mumbled, "Wow, I am a terrible father ..."

We may not like where we find ourselves, but once we become aware of the truth and confront it honestly, we are in a position to grow and change if we so choose.

Living with your values in mind, and making sure your actions are in line with your values, will set you up for personal growth, self-confidence, and respect from others with similar values. You will be making a clear statement to those you interact with daily; you will be creating Life Momentum.

The Brain on Personal Values

~Amy Guy

REALLY? WE ACTUALLY HAVE to write down that we will tell the truth, that we will be trustworthy, and that we will be honest? Don't we just automatically practice these behaviors without having to specifically make a commitment on paper? Well, actually, no, we don't.

I have spent the last fifteen-plus years working with people to help them in their quest to lead successful and satisfying lives. What I find is, at the root of many psychological issues, people act inconsistently with their beliefs. They profess to one thing, but their behaviors run counter to those beliefs. They mentally rationalize these actions in ways that allow them to remain unaware of the damage they are inflicting on themselves. These mental maneuverings drain their energy and interfere with their connections to self, coworkers, and loved ones.

Numerous studies have been done in recent years showing the percentage of high school students who cheat. Many studies indicate up to 95% of high school students admit to some form of cheating. In my work, I have the opportunity to meet many high school kids. I began to ask them about these startling statistics. Their assessments were not comforting. Almost everyone knows that cheating is wrong. However, once we begin to tell ourselves that we are "not really cheating" or "it's no big deal" or "everyone is doing it", we set up a pattern of rationalization, diminishing our positive energy and the chance for a healthy connection with other people. Awareness is crucial if we are to begin to live out our statement of personal integrity. We ought not go through life blindly, lacking compassion and empathy for others whose lives we impact.

From a psychological perspective, the root of integrity is compassion for others and the understanding that our behaviors produce ripples affecting ourselves and others. We must be disciplined and deliberate in our awareness of our behaviors.

On a personal level, I find the Rotary Four Way Test helpful in gauging my own values in various situations. The test includes the following:

1. Is it the TRUTH?
2. Is it FAIR to all concerned?
3. Will it build GOODWILL and BETTER FRIENDSHIPS?
4. Will it be BENEFICIAL to all involved?

As a member of Rotary International, I recite these points every week with my fellow Rotarians. I cannot emphasize strongly enough what the impact of asking these questions has had on my behavior. Now, without even thinking about them, I feel how deeply they have become a part of who I am.

The more we affirm and repeat our statement of personal integrity, the more likely we are to find ourselves living by it. From a brain perspective, many times we are faced with a decision, the decision arises from the visceral, or emotional, part of the brain. When we are working from this part of the brain, we are not considering the long-term consequences of our behavior. It is more about doing what feels good in that moment.

When we have a statement of personal integrity that we see and use as a daily affirmation to ourselves, we have brain circuitry in place that helps us make decisions from this point, and not from an emotional place that can be inconsistent with our values.

Helpful Examples of Personal Values

My values are honesty, trustworthiness, awareness, competitiveness, and balance.

I live a balanced and honest life. I can count on myself, and others can count on me to get the job done well and on time.

I live a sincere, patient life with others' needs in mind.

I live with enthusiasm fueled by my growth and the growth of others.

Personal growth, awareness, honesty, patience help me live a balanced life.

I live my life with reason as my guide.

My family and friends can count on me to be sincere, understanding, and loving. I will be there when they need me.

WORDS TO CONSIDER IN CREATING YOUR PERSONAL VALUES STATEMENT:

Awareness	Honesty
Passion	Change
Growth	Accountable
Confidence	Consistency
Reason	Responsible
Effectiveness	Commitment
Mindfulness	Trust
Vision	Timeliness
Open Mindedness	Making a difference
Thoughtfulness	Persistence

Chapter Five

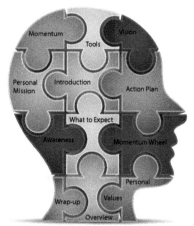

Awareness Overview

Working definition of Awareness:

AWARENESS IS YOUR HONEST, informed knowledge or perception of the facts or situations that make up your life. Awareness is only possible with honesty to one's self.

Awareness is the key to growth and change.

~Author unknown

Awareness Introduction

SO, THERE ARE THESE two guys, and each one is in a deep hole—about four feet deeper than they are tall. Which guy is in trouble and which guy is in a good place? One guy is good looking, well educated, and wealthy and isn't aware, or won't admit, he is in a hole. The other guy is average looking with an average job and a high school education, but he knows he is in a hole. Which guy is better off? Which guy knows enough to start climbing?

"Awareness is the key to growth and change." This simple quote packs a wallop. How many times have you seen or heard friends or family in self-denial, unaware of what is obvious to you and others? Are there important aspects of your life where you are lacking awareness? I have certainly worked on this to better my life and, along the way, have encouraged others to do the same.

On one occasion, I had a very blunt discussion with a friend, encouraging him to work on his self-awareness. My friend is a very talented guy in many ways, but much of the success and joy in his life were being drowned out by the parts of his life he was unaware of or just chose to ignore. He had lived for so many years in this state of unawareness, of not being honest with the fact he was in a deep hole, that it took great courage and energy just to start the climb out.

More than a couple of times, he called me up and claimed that this newfound awareness was going to kill him.

My friend's story ends happily. He was finally able to climb out of that hole. I often asked him during his struggles, which was harder: living in the hole unaware, being in the hole with awareness, or the climb out. What do you think he said?

Think back to something in your life that you became aware of for the first time. What did you do with the newfound awareness? I hope that you climbed out of that deep dark place once you were aware of it. I hope the experience encouraged you to work even harder on awareness throughout your life.

It is unfortunate that so many people stay with what they know. If they do become aware, they don't really know what to do about it. Whether we dug in consciously or not, somehow we get remarkably comfortable in that hole. It is well documented that some people who serve long prison sentences are either hesitant to leave or don't want to leave at all.

To many of you, I have good news. Although awareness can be a bit overwhelming at first, it is the key to change and personal growth. The rewards awaiting you are far more desirable than the cold comfort of the status quo.

The Brain on Awareness

~Amy Guy

AWARENESS IS FUNDAMENTAL TO mental health. The word awareness is used consistently throughout the Life Momentum lessons for that very reason. It is the foundation for all other actions. Utilizing awareness as the first tool out of your toolbox will help you connect to and act upon feelings, ideas, and situations you deal with every day. A lack of awareness is apparent when we take in and absorb only the information we think we can tolerate. This is your brain protecting you from information or realities you are not prepared to face.

The opposite of awareness is avoidance, a familiar and ineffective coping tactic. One of my favorite researchers, therapist John Briere, writes about the "pain paradox". Briere puts forth the idea that the more we avoid things, the less pain we have. This tactic actually fosters more pain in the long run, though. Briere continues this theme by pointing out the optimal avoidance of pain (meaning you can avoid enough to get through your day) can be useful for a period of time and in some circumstances, but you also have to begin making progress on what it is you are avoiding. This is where the *Awareness* tool comes into play.

On a personal note, before I discovered the Dave Ramsey FPU online program, Financial Peace University, I was adept at avoidance when it came to money issues. I had no idea what I spent my money on or why I never seemed to have enough! On a scale of 1 to 10, my awareness was zero. After working the Ramsey program, I adopted an "envelope system" (visually handling and seeing where my money was going), and my awareness jumped to 10. I knew where EVERY dollar of my paycheck was going. I HATED THIS! It was so hard for me. I was angry and grouchy about it. It reminded me of my childhood, being raised by my very frugal parents. The newfound awareness was difficult to accept, and I was very uncomfortable with it. However, eventually I became aware of how much I had been avoiding my financial responsibilities and realized what a huge mess I had to clean up. I finally accepted the notion that avoidance actually does cause more pain than awareness.

Similar situations may occur when it comes to any of the categories on the Momentum Wheel, which will be introduced in the following pages.

According to neuroscience, the basal ganglia are the home of implicit (unspoken) learning, and of intuition. This gut feeling, as it is often called, is experienced in body and mind. One cannot accurately articulate intuition. Some choose to act on this feeling, while others choose to ignore it. Once again, we are presented with the avoidance versus awareness situation. Without the ability to pay attention to our own body and become aware of our feelings, we do not have the tools to tap into this thing called intuition.

Daniel Goleman, psychologist and scientific journalist, describes the basal ganglia as the area of the brain that observes everything we do in life, every situation we may face.

Our life wisdom on any topic is stored in the basal ganglia. This part of the brain is so primitive it has zero connectivity to the verbal cortex. It can't tell us what it knows in words; it tells us in feelings. Because the basal ganglia have a great deal of connectivity to the emotional centers of the brain, it . tells us, in our gut, what is right and what is wrong.

Sometimes the brain tries to protect us from pain and we become anxious. Our reaction comes from the emotional part of the brain (limbic system), and we don't see things clearly. Therefore, we cannot really be aware of things as they truly are. To be aware of things, we must quiet our busy minds enough to actually see what is going on. Awareness takes time and focus. Awareness and avoidance are on a continuum.

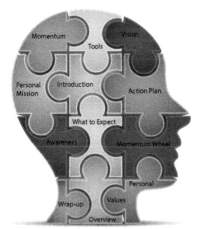

Momentum Wheel Overview

Working definition of The Momentum Wheel:

THE MOMENTUM WHEEL IS a tool to display the pieces of our lives and how these pieces interact with each other. The Momentum Wheel promotes an honest and aware view of every piece of your life as well as your plans and priorities for each piece.

Momentum Wheel Introduction

MY FAMILY IS VERY important to me. They are my top priority. My social time and my health are important, as is my time for church and my continuing education. Just writing down all these areas of my life that need my personal attention makes me anxious. I need more time to relax. How can a person fit everything in? Are some parts of your life going great and others falling apart?

I clearly recall the lack of balance in my life as a college student. I was very good at leisure and social activities. I had a good job, so my finances and career were on track. A golf scholarship took care of my tuition. I was doing great! I enjoyed the rigid practice schedule necessary to keep my scholarship, but one major part of this scenario was heading south. My falling grades were beginning to upset the perfect little world I had created. Each time I fell behind in my schoolwork, my golf game suffered, which caused me to worry about staying on the team. A vicious cycle began to take hold: worry that my father would be angry over my poor grades, worry that I would lose my scholarship, worry that I would flunk out altogether. Even my girlfriend was getting on my nerves and we weren't getting along. This total imbalance would not fly with my father, and it certainly wasn't acceptable to me.

Fast-forward ten years. At my mother's urging, my new wife and I attended a series of classes designed to help couples secure a positive future for their marriage. The facilitator was Dr. Ford, a very experienced psychologist who focused on the difference between spoken priorities and lived priorities. The part of the class that made the biggest impression on us revolved around an exercise whereby one of the men in the audience listed a number of priorities in his life on a blackboard.

It was your average list: family, wife, religion, career, health, finances, friends, dog. Dr. Ford then asked the man a series of questions. How many hours a week do you work? How many hours a week do you participate in activities with your friends or on your own? How much time do you spend with your kids, the whole family, your wife, the dog, etc. The man was able to easily answer all the questions.

After all the questions were answered, Dr. Ford wrote the same list, but in a different order than that of the original list. This list went like this: career, friends, kids, religion, health, dog, wife. As Dr. Ford was completing this list, a faint sobbing could be heard from the first row.

Dr. Ford explained that the first list reflected the man's spoken values priority order. The second list, written by Dr. Ford, reflected the lived values priority order. The sobbing in the front row grew louder. Dr. Ford and the husband had a short conversation. The husband was incensed by the doctor's remarks and insisted his wife and family were the top priority in his life. His wife's sobbing told a much different story.

There are so many issues that cause imbalance in our lives. The good things we are doing get overshadowed by the parts of our lives with which we are struggling. We might be doing great with our careers but not taking care of our health, becoming run-down or ill. Parents say they can't take care of themselves because they give 100% of their efforts to their children. The parent seems sincere, even noble, but if *you* are not 100% how can you *give* 100%? Obviously, you don't want to model poor health for your children either.

Balance is important, but how do we achieve it? This is the heavy lifting part of Life Momentum. Let us lay out a plan to address all parts of your life that you consider important, and see how you can make it all work. Yes, it is possible! You will refer to your mission statement, vision statement, and stated values with complete honesty in order to broaden your awareness and allow yourself to make and commit to the decisions you will need in this lesson. The only way to build sustainable momentum in your life is with deep, thoughtful, reflective, soul-searching honesty as your sword to cut through all the half-truths, lies, avoidance techniques, and anything else you use to insulate yourself.

I have a couple of questions to leave with you while you work on the ten most valued pieces of your life. Can you trust yourself if you are not honest with yourself or others? Can you trust others if you are not honest? Is there awareness without honesty? I can answer the last one for you. NOT A CHANCE. Remember that the hole you are in is far worse than the climb out will be.

We have tools to help those who choose to make the climb and create momentum in their lives.

Here are the ten pieces of the Momentum Wheel. These pieces of your life are essential and universal to all human beings:

1. Physical Health
2. Mental Health
3. Career
4. Education/Personal Development
5. Family
6. Marriage/Relationships
7. Finances
8. Community
9. Friends/Social/Fun & Leisure Activities
10. Spirituality

As you review, evaluate, and analyze these pieces of your life, consider this: All of our priorities are important. They absolutely fit together and affect each other. However, it is essential to realize that your newfound awareness of these connections is, in itself, a big step. Life isn't a game of perfection. It's all about being aware, improving, and moving from where you are toward where you want to be. It may be that you are in a place in your life that makes it difficult to take on all of these issues at once. Start where you are now; do what you can. It's all about being aware, improving, and moving from where you are toward where you want to be. It's about getting started!

Creating an Awareness Exercise

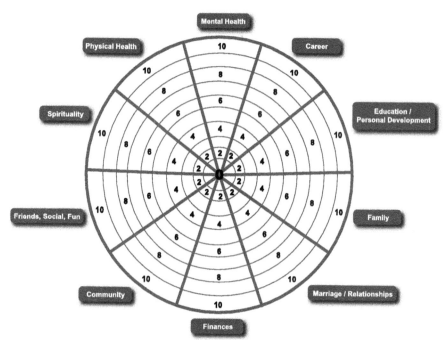

FILL IN THE AREAS from 1–10 to indicate your current level of awareness in each of the pieces of your life. Number 1 would indicate least satisfied, number 10 most satisfied. You will not spend the same time on each piece of your life, but understanding how the pieces overlap is very important.

The Momentum Wheel will help you track the changes in each piece of your life as you fill out the chart on a monthly or quarterly basis. The key is to be aware of all pieces of your life and manage the low priority pieces so that areas that require more attention are not negatively affected.

- Understand that each area of your life needs to be considered to achieve balance.
- Utilize this awareness activity to analyze each area of your life.
- Be aware of your strengths and the opportunities available to you.
- See the areas of your life that are problematic and need to be addressed.
- Identify action plans for each area of your life.

Regular use of the Awareness Exercise Wheel will show you where you are at any given time and where you specifically need to focus attention. This exercise will help you to successfully manage your life.

Chapter Six

Physical Health Introduction

Mental Health Introduction

Career Introduction

Education/Personal Development Introduction

Family Introduction

Physical Health Introduction

I always believed that exercise is the key not only to physical health but to peace of mind

~Nelson Mandela

WALKING, JOGGING, HIKING, AND maintaining a proper diet won't cost you any extra money. You will even save money when you avoid buying the high-priced junk foods on the market.

Both the medical and science communities clearly promote good physical health. The one argument we hear, which you may have said it yourself is, "I don't have time." You don't have time to stay healthy? Actually, you can't afford not to be healthy. Yes, it may take an hour or so out of your day to eat properly and exercise, but the benefits derived in renewed energy, a more positive outlook, and an all-around sense of well-being are priceless.

The fact that you are reading this book is evidence that you are willing to take some big steps in learning to live your life with momentum. You know you will be challenged. Do what you can to prepare for that challenge.

Your Action Plan is ready for you. Get strong and stay strong. Make certain you are ready for it!

The Brain & Body on Physical Health

~Amy Guy

A PHYSICAL WORKOUT IS an amazing activity. As you begin exercising, your brain cells immediately start functioning at a higher level. This increase in function aids in focus and sustained energy throughout an entire day. That's the good part. The not-so-good part is that not all of us work out regularly. Just as any other discipline requires consistency to attain success, so too does physical activity.

When you work out regularly, your brain gets used to the frequent surges of blood and adapts to that surge by turning certain genes on or off. Many of these subtle changes boost brain cell function and protect against diseases such as Alzheimer's, Parkinson's, and even stroke. According to a study by the Department of Exercise Science at the University of Georgia, even exercising for twenty minutes a day facilitates information processing and memory functions.

Your brain is no different than the rest of the muscles in your body. As the saying goes, "use it or lose it." You know that physical exercise stimulates growth of muscle cells, but do you know exercise also stimulates brain plasticity by promoting growth of new connections between cells in the cortical areas of the brains. We all know people "hooked" on running or other strenuous exercise. What motivates someone to work so hard? What's the payoff?

Various forms of exercise provide a burst of serotonin, a chemical created by the human body. Working as a neurotransmitter, serotonin influences—directly and indirectly—the majority of brain cells. The result is a feeling of wellbeing and happiness, which helps maintain mood balance. And balance is what momentum building is all about.

Real-life Examples

~Amy Guy

THE SINGLE MOST IMPORTANT thing I do every day of my life is to go for a run. Running has made my life what it is today. How can this be, you ask? Running on a regular basis provides the momentum with which I have accomplished things that I would not have thought possible.

My love affair with running began when I signed up for my first 5K. My plan was to combine walking and running with friends. I didn't think I could possibly run the entire distance. As luck would have it, or maybe it was fate, someone I really didn't want to beat me passed me up! I darted away from my friends, turned up the heat, and ended up passing my competitor right before the finish line. I was hooked! Two months later I registered for a half marathon (13.1 miles). A year later I entered a full marathon. I found myself spending more and more time with other runners and running on a daily basis. Every activity or mission has a better outcome when I run. I do my work better, I interact with people in a more positive and energized manner, and I talk better to myself.

This positive feedback fuels the desire to run, and the running turns up my energy level in all parts of my life. Each time I complete a long run, I am reminded that anything is possible and that I am capable of far more than I give myself credit for. I know not everyone can run marathons, but everyone can do some sort of physical activity. Start small and build from a light workout to a more strenuous regimen. The key is the regularity of the activity. There is a tendency to go all out a couple of times and then drop the plan.

Stick with a program, and you will find your body is capable of more than you thought. You might even start enjoying it! Exercise teaches you how to work through pain rather than letting it stop you in your tracks. I believe a strong mind equals a strong body. As you strengthen your body, your mind becomes stronger. It's a beautiful relationship: strong body=strong mind; strong mind=strong body. Try it!

Physical Health Awareness Review

REMEMBER, BEING PHYSICALLY ACTIVE
ALLOWS YOU TO:

- Enjoy good health
- Increase your chances of living longer
- Maintain a good self-image
- Avoid depression
- Sleep better at night
- Keep bones and muscles strong

REMEMBER, STAYING PHYSICALLY FIT HELPS
REDUCE RISKS FOR:

- Heart disease; Stroke; High blood pressure
- Type 2 diabetes; Obesity; Depression
- Breast and colon cancer; Osteoporosis

Mental Health Introduction

DO YOU STRUGGLE WITH a sense of being over-whelmed? Do you find yourself down in the dumps due to low energy? Is your stress level shutting down your ability to think and be creative enough to handle life's daily challenges? It is possible for you to confront these negative mental health issues and turn them into positives.

A person's physical health is closely aligned with his or her mental health. Here again the science is clear: Good physical health sets you up for good mental health.

The tools we use, including *Ideas and Issues, Awareness,* and the Action Plan, have all proven to be helpful in improving a person's outlook on life. The act of addressing all areas of one's life, becoming more aware of specific issues, and committing oneself to action can and will reduce stress and confusion. With a healthy mental attitude, creative and physical energy become available means for meeting challenges and reaching goals.

The Brain on Mental Health

~Amy Guy

MICHELLE GIELAN, FOUNDER OF the Institute for Applied Positive Research, is an expert in the science of long-term happiness and human potential. Research shows that 90% of our long-term happiness is determined NOT by external circumstances, but rather by how we process the world around us! In other words, there is a correlation between a positive brain and good mental health and success in all facets of one's life.

You are no doubt familiar with the puzzle, "Is a half glass of water half full or half empty?" As with many things in life, it depends on how you look at any given situation. A pessimist tends to see only the difficult aspects of new opportunities. An optimist, on the other hand, sees the opportunity in difficulties.

The key to becoming more optimistic starts with changing the relationship you have with your thoughts. If you change your thoughts by looking at the upside rather than the downside of situations, you can actually change your feelings and how you view various circumstances. Through practice, you can learn to be more positive, more grateful, and happier overall.

Try working through the balance wheel by putting into practice the feelings of optimism and gratitude that will help you to live a balanced life. You will take comfort in seeing the world clearly rather than through a skewed vision or a tornado of emotions. The connection between a positive brain and success in business, health, and relationships cannot be denied.

Real-life Examples

~John Perles

ON A PERSONAL NOTE, I have come to realize that the benefits I gain by following a healthy regimen have a positive effect on my mental health, as well as on my physical health. Regular exercise and a healthy diet appear to be as important to my ability to concentrate, maintain a pleasing attitude, and exhibit self-control as they are to my physical well-being. Without fail, every time I neglect my regular physical workouts I let my diet deteriorate, and my normally positive outlook on life becomes erratic or even negative. It is obvious that when I let one part of my life slide, other areas of my life will surely suffer.

Strange as it may seem, robust regular physical activity makes a person more energetic, while avoidance of physical activity makes a person lethargic. The downward spiral continues. Though I feel tired, I do not sleep well. My level of patience goes down, and irritability begins to rear its head. As I tell my clients, the time you take out of your day to perform your workout regimen will, in the long run, be less time than the time gained by being energetic and productive.

Not only will you become more accomplished, your overall attitude will be better, and you will actually enjoy what you are doing. It cannot be stressed enough that each of us has more control over our mental health than we think we do. Barring the existence of a diagnosed mental illness, it is imperative that we become aware of changes in our daily activities that tend to bring us down mentally and emotionally.

The need for structure in one's life is essential. Like a well-oiled piece of machinery, our physical and mental health will thrive when we operate on a steady routine. Virtually every time I engage a new client, I detect stress, fatigue, even a sense of isolation. Overwhelmed, the client exhibits differing levels of depression and even hopelessness. More often than not, there are physical issues of some sort at the root of this emotional imbalance. I came to realize that most of the individuals I describe share several traits: the failure to create and maintain a strong foundation for their businesses or their lives in general, no stated purpose; no specific direction, no obvious structure, no tools with which to build these components so necessary to a successful business or personal life.

It is possible to turn stress into success by getting honest with yourself. Define your purpose and your vision. Develop and execute an Action Plan to take you from where you are to where you want to be. Over time, the strongest among us will fall ill, act out of character, or simply want to give up. The beauty is, in most cases you can take action to bring relief. As with all growth, improving mental health begins with honesty and awareness, which leads to a workable plan.

Mental Health Awareness Review

GOOD MENTAL HEALTH ISN'T just the absence of mental health problems. Many of the following characteristics are likely to be present in individuals with good mental health:

- A sense of well-being and contentment
- A zest for living—the ability to enjoy life, to laugh and have fun
- Resiliency—being able to deal with life's stresses and bounce back from adversity
- Self-realization—participating in life to the fullest extent possible, through meaningful activities and positive relationships
- Flexibility—the ability to change, grow, and experience a range of feelings as life's circumstances change
- A sense of balance in one's life—between solitude and sociability, work and play, sleep and wakefulness, rest and exercise, etc.
- A sense of well-roundedness—with attention to mind, body, spirit, creativity, intellectual development, health, etc.
- The ability to care for oneself and for others
- Self-confidence and good self-esteem

Career Introduction

About one third of our lives are spent working. Our work spills over into our personal lives and often shapes who we are as well as who we spend time with. It is very difficult, if not impossible to have a work life balance if you are demotivated, frustrated, and feel like you are wasting your time at work. Chances are much of your social time will be spent worrying about or complaining about your job which can affect your physical health as well as your relationships with family and friends.

~Steve Jobs

DO YOU THINK OF the work you do as a job or as a career? Do you gain personal satisfaction from your work over and above the livelihood it provides? Will your career path lead you to a broadening of life experiences and provide the incentive to broaden your knowledge of your chosen field? My father always said, "You should love your work and be properly compensated, in that order." In other words, love what you do and the money will follow.

Over the course of my career, I have seen many people struggle to find satisfaction in their work. According to a Gallup poll, 90% of the workforce is disengaged or unhappy at work. Becoming one of those who is actively engaged requires awareness. Awareness begins with an honest assessment. Take the time to assess where you are and where you want to be on your career path.

Ask yourself a few basic questions. Do you look forward to going to work most days, or do you merely tolerate your job? Are you satisfied with your salary? Does the work you do build or undermine your confidence? The way you view your career affects your feelings of self-worth, your lifestyle, plans for retirement, and networking opportunities. With these points in mind, make an honest assessment of the current state of your career.

The Brain on Career

~Amy Guy

"BY WHAT AGE DO you think I will hate my job?" Imagine my shock at hearing these words from a junior high student. What could possibly cause someone so young to imagine such a dire and unsatisfying future? Why would someone automatically assume that with a career comes misery and disappointment?

Almost without exception, each of us will hold a job at some time in our lives. Most people will settle on a career path that will carry them through to an age of retirement. As with all endeavors, the opportunity for success is measured by the sense of meaning and purpose intrinsic to that endeavor. Whatever employment you decide on, know that, for your own well-being, a paycheck alone will not provide a sense of fulfillment and satisfaction.

You will have a number of different employment positions throughout your life. Each step should be well considered and carefully thought out. It is an important aspect of your life, but it is not the only aspect. Whatever career choice you make, it must mesh with other aspects of your life.

Are you excited and enthusiastic about your work? Do you look forward to going to work? Are you motivated to excel at ever-increasing levels? Do you find the challenges in your work stimulating? Do you find purpose in your field of employment? It is said: Do what you love and the money will come. Is your career on the path you envision? Dr. David Bennett, Director of Memory and Aging at Rush Medical Center in Chicago, contends that people who have meaning and purpose in their lives have a lower risk for cognitive impairment in later life. Furthermore, purpose in life is linked to many positive outcomes: better mental health, happiness, satisfaction, personal growth, and longevity. A career affects all parts of one's life: personal confidence, lifestyle, retirement plans, social networking, to name only a few areas. *Your Life Is Your Business* is an excellent resource for pinpointing and dealing with the various aspects of your life as they impact your chosen career.

Real-life Examples

IF YOU ADD UP the time you spend commuting to work, preparing for work, actually being at work, and the time you think about your work, you soon realize that work-related activities occupy most of your waking hours.

Do you work for someone else? Is your career in your own hands or under someone else's control? Do you have a long-range plan for your career? What do you want from your career, other than a paycheck?

This is a story about a young woman with whom I consult. She has pursued several different careers. She has always been regarded as smart, hardworking, a great team player, and very effective in her various positions. However, she tends not to promote herself. It wasn't in her makeup to ask for a raise or seek a promotion. She was content giving all of the power to others. Her salary was nominal. She was more or less satisfied with her jobs, so she accepted the status quo.

She and I discussed her overall financial status in terms of retirement and financial security. Once we started to get to the facts, her mood changed. Clearly, she was struggling with both her career path and her finances. All of a sudden, she was less than thrilled with her career path and her current job. Nothing except her awareness had changed, but that was more than enough to prompt her to examine her current situation. She started to think in terms of what she wanted her future to be.

Simply taking the time to write down her current income and what was necessary for both her short-term spending and long-term savings goals was enough to get the ball rolling. This woman realized that her career decisions, her reluctance to be proactive, and her hesitancy to discuss salary issues had all worked against her personal financial well-being. She came to the decision that any discomfort that might result from her speaking up and acting on her own behalf would be the lesser of the two evils. She saw the merit of developing a plan to help her get on a positive, goal-oriented life path.

This is how she began:

1. I need to make more money.
2. I want to enjoy my job and the people with whom I work.
3. I prefer a job that incorporates a physical aspect.
4. I want a job that provides some flexibility in the work schedule.
5. I want to know that the quality of work, when it exceeds all expectations, will be financially acknowledged.

Great start! Now what? We began by discussing and identifying companies and positions that would meet her criteria. I impressed on her that this process would take time. In addition, and more importantly, the process would take her out of her comfort zone. She would need to promote herself to people she had never met.

Would her current job qualify as a potential candidate? She liked the people, and she liked the work. The negative factors revolved around finances. She would need a salary of 30%–40% higher than she was currently receiving. The story doesn't end there. In fact, it gets better; the result was a win-win situation. The company's owner had been trying to retire, or cut back on his workweek, for some time. He had even considered selling the company. Easier said than done!

This is where our newly inspired young lady approached her boss, the company's owner. She told him she had a plan to help him meet his challenges, while, at the same time, her financial concerns must be met. Problems solved! It turned out to be an easy decision, as her employer just had never thought of that arrangement. Wow! Isn't it amazing what a sense of awareness can accomplish? Naturally, problems won't always be solved this quickly and smoothly, but how will you know if you don't get started?

Career Awareness Review

DO YOU WANT A job or a career? Is there a difference? The subtle difference between a job and a career is that a job is something you do for the money, and a career is work you do because you care about the results.

A career is a series of connected employment opportunities. You will continually build up skills to move you into ever-higher-paying positions. In five years, you're planning to be doing something similar to what you're doing now, but with more income and more interesting problems to tackle. A career provides a foundation of experiences and learning that will fuel your professional life.

Are you investing the time and energy required for establishing a career? Are you making workplace connections and putting yourself in positions for promotions and salary increases? The career path requires that you go that extra mile and make that extra effort.

To begin to create a personal career development plan, you must first determine your destination. Follow this with a gap analysis: Where you are now versus where you want to be.

Education/Personal Development Introduction

Develop a passion for learning. If you do, you will never cease to grow.

~Anthony J. D'Angelo, founder Collegiate Empowerment

IN TODAY'S WORLD, IT is easier than ever to become well educated. The United States has the largest public education system in the world. Modern technology, specifically the Internet, makes vast amounts of information available to all. The use of computers is available to everyone, regardless of economic status. Public libraries provide computers for public use at no charge. Libraries provide a wealth of information and services.

Educating yourself prepares you for the opportunities that present themselves throughout your life. One cannot predict when and where occasions for entrance to, or advancement in, a particular field may become available. Being ready and able to take advantage of these opportunities is up to you. The avenues available for learning are many and varied. Online classes on any subject imaginable are available at a reasonable cost and at a time convenient to the user. Websites that emphasize the importance of a classical education provide online lectures on topics such as great literature, politics, and philosophy, to name a few.

Community organizations provide a great setting for expanding one's knowledge. Belonging to and supporting community activities is a win-win situation. Sharing ideas, developing projects, solving problems, and learning to build coalitions serve to broaden the horizons of all concerned. Give yourself the gift of learning. Become aware of the abundance of learning opportunities available and take advantage of them. The objective of *Your Life Is Your Business* is to help you to help yourself. The objective is to put YOU in the driver's seat and in control of your own life.

The Brain on Education/Personal Development

~Amy Guy

Anyone who stops learning is old, whether 20 or 80. Anyone who keeps learning stays young. The greatest thing in life is to keep your mind young.

~Henry Ford

THE BRAIN CHANGES CONSTANTLY as a result of learning and remains "plastic" throughout life. Neuroscience has shown that learning a new skill (juggling, playing an instrument, taking up a new sport, etc.) changes the brain and that those changes revert back when we stop practicing the skill. This is what is meant by "Use it or lose it." Only those connections and pathways that are activated frequently are kept. Other connections that aren't used will become extinct.

This is why learning new things exercises your brain and strengthens connections. There has been a great deal of research recently regarding brain fitness. Websites that promote these ideas, such as Lumosity, an online brain training and neuroscience research company based in San Francisco, California.

challenge us to do brain exercises on a regular schedule, just as we do with physical exercise. We know that by simply shaking up the monotony of daily activities we can trigger our brain to use different pathways and grow new connections. Consider brushing your teeth with your non-dominant hand. You'd better plan on it taking a little longer than usual!

Real-life Examples

ONE OF THE GREATEST personal pleasures I derive from my consulting work is being able to help companies create a culture that promotes the personal growth of its employees. In some cases, the strides made in this direction are substantial; in other situations, less so. What is most important, however, is that through education and incremental improvements, individuals develop a more positive view of their potential. Without this attitude, it is easy to fall behind those who do see success in their future. Failure to reach one's full potential is a loss to all. The fact that you are participating in *Your Life Is Your Business* indicates you are motivated and ready to take the path necessary to achieve your goals.

Companies that provide a nurturing culture see their employees flourish. There are many stories of individuals returning to college to earn advanced degrees. Others take on responsibilities over and above their job description in order to move up one or two rungs of the ladder. The drive in these people comes from an awareness of what is required to succeed, and a willingness to change in order for that success to be achieved.

Let me share a simple, but great, story of a waitress I will call Annie. Everyone liked Annie, and Annie tried very hard to do her job well. When monthly performance reviews were instituted at the restaurant where she was employed, Annie was in trouble. This was the first time in Annie's life that she was able to make a good salary, work in a good environment, and work with people she liked. The reviews showed her sales per customer numbers to be too low. Her appearance was not up to par. Worst of all, her ability to face her challenges and take control of her life were sorely lacking.

This was a critical moment for Annie. Would she use this information provided in her review as constructive criticism, becoming aware of the issues holding her down and working to correct them, or would she deny the facts laid out before her?

Fortunately, Annie was open to the idea of improving. The company gave her the extra training she needed and even assigned a young lady who recently found herself on a similar path to mentor Annie. The first step was for Annie to survive the two-week mandatory time to hit measured improvement goals. Annie made it! The second step was to show she could sustain the improvements and progress even further. Less than two months later, Annie was second in sales per customer in the entire restaurant.

I happened to be in the restaurant about this time. I didn't need to see the sales numbers to know how she was doing. I saw the confidence in her walk and a dramatic improvement in her personal appearance and strong body language when interacting with her customers.

Good for you, Annie. You let the review and its constructive criticism serve to raise your awareness. You had the courage to make the necessary changes that will help you, far beyond the restaurant venue. The energy and challenge necessary for Annie to change was far less taxing than what she would have faced had she not changed. Growth comes from awareness. A great company culture and sincere, thoughtful people help a bunch, too.

Education/Personal Development Awareness Review

CONSIDER TAKING SMALL, BUT regular steps to expand your personal development and education to live a fuller, more balanced life. Begin by diversifying your experiences. Skip the usual Saturday night blockbuster movie and take in a lecture on the art of filmmaking.

Don't fear change; embrace it. Engage in community activities. Volunteer to work on the stage crew for the next local playhouse performance.

Try new foods. Consider eating at a different ethnic restaurant once a month. Do some traveling; it doesn't have to be anything grandiose. Motor to a nearby city and learn how it got its name, find out what it has to offer, what makes people want to live there.

The more we open ourselves to new experiences, to meeting new people, and confronting new challenges, the more enjoyable and rich our lives become.

Family Introduction

I think togetherness is a very important ingredient to family life.

~Barbara Bush

JUST THE WORD FAMILY evokes many emotions. Family might be the hardest part of your life to examine and the most important to understand. Do you have enough quality time with your family? Do you look forward to family gatherings? How would you describe the quality of your conversations with family members? Is your family an asset or a liability in your life? If you could change three things in your relationship with your family or a family member what would they be?

Imagine yourself in the place of a family member. Consider the hurdles that person may be facing; think of ways to show understanding; share delight in the good fortune of another as well as concern for misfortunes.

The life skills you hone in other areas of your life will help you navigate the ups and downs that come with family. Your personal demeanor, understanding, and thoughtful reactions may well provide a model for others in your family.

The Brain on Family

~Amy Guy

WHEN ONE HEARS THE word family, many things come to mind. Some of us would list our family as the number one priority in our lives. Most of us are aware that the most precious gift we can give our family is time. Why is it then that a lot of us struggle to make enough time for those people who matter most to us? In my years as a therapist, I have seen many people struggle to fill the different roles they play in their families. I have counseled many individuals who would list family as a difficult aspect of their lives.

We all have a family. Some of us have a different definition of what family actually is. There seems to be pressure to be the perfect mother, father, spouse, daughter, son, etc. We live in a culture where no matter how much we accomplish it never seems to be enough. Because of social media, we are constantly comparing our family moments with our friends' family moments. We must remind ourselves that there is no way to be a perfect spouse, mother, or father, etc. There are, however, a million ways to be a *good* one!

According to happiness researchers, there is no stronger predictor of happiness than how close and connected we feel with other people. Professor of Psychology at Harvard University, Daniel Gilbert, points to the fact that people are happy when they have family and friends. When you think of the things that make you happy, they often involve even more ways of getting more family ends.

So, there is research to prove that spending time with family is crucial to mental well-being and happiness. Not staying in touch with friends and family is one of the top-five regrets cited when a death occurs. What are you waiting for? PICK UP THE PHONE and connect with someone you love.

Real-life Examples

~Amy Guy

SOMEONE ONCE TOLD ME, "A man without a vision for his future always returns to his past."

My work puts me in contact with many young people. In these encounters, the issue of family is a key topic of discussion. Those who experience their actual family in an unpleasant light work hard to create the family they wish they had.

An exercise I recommend to my audience is one in which each individual lists those aspects of his or her birth family they would bring to new relationships and which aspects they would reject.

When reflecting on negative feelings surrounding your birth family, it is helpful to look to the generation in which your parents were raised. We learn how to parent from our own parents. This observation doesn't change how you feel, but it does provide insight that you can use to avoid repeating those behaviors you found objectionable, and reinforcing those that were of a positive nature.

This is the part of our work where we have to get real. We each have parts of our lives that we prefer to let be. For many reasons, we resist the change that would be required if we did choose to address certain issues. However, whether or not to face these matters is a personal decision.

There is an important caveat to consider. It is important to make sure you are as fully aware as possible of the matters and the facts involved. You cannot honestly decide on whether or not to act if you don't have complete awareness and understanding of the specifics.

Current generations have the advantage of a great many studies and writings on the topic of family. There is no shortage of worthwhile information available. What could possibly be more important than growing up in an emotionally healthy family? It is in your power to resist repeating past mistakes. Having a keen awareness of your situation and a well-thought-out vision of what you want your own family to be will help you to create that family.

Family Relationships Awareness Review

FIVE "L'S" OF POSITIVE family relationships:

Learning—Families are where we learn values, skills, and behavior.

Loyalty—Strong families have a sense of loyalty and devotion toward family members. The family sticks together. They stand by each other during times of trouble. They stand up for each other when attacked by someone outside the family.

Love—Love is at the heart of the family. All humans have the need to love and to be loved; the family is normally the place where love is expressed.

Laughter—Laughter is good family medicine. Humor is an escape valve for family tension. Through laughter we learn to see ourselves honestly and objectively.

Leadership—Leadership is essential. Family members, usually the adults, must assume responsibility for leading the family. If no one accepts this vital role, the family will weaken. Each family needs its own special set of rules and guidelines.

Chapter Seven

Marriage and Relationships Introduction

Finances Introduction

Community Introduction

Friends, Social, and Fun Introduction

Spirituality Introduction

Marriage and Relationships Introduction

Happily ever after is not a fairy tale, it is a choice.

How are you and your better half doing? Is yours a supportive, flourishing relationship? How would you rate your skills in communicating? Do you spend quality time together? Do your spoken priorities match the way you live your life?

It is safe to say that most relationships have an ebb and flow quality. Our most important relationships need the time and attention of review and reflection, just like the other priorities in our life. With a clear, complete picture of your relationship, the communication between you and your partner will be more constructive and effective. I encourage you and your partner to attempt to see situations from each other's perspective.

Ask yourself this question: Do my actions and words empower and support my partner? Is it ever an advantage to you or your partner to negatively impact the other? It is sometimes the case that what we say is not what our partner actually hears. Successful marriages and relationships require time, attention, patience, and love.

The Brain on Marriage and Relationships

~Amy Guy

ONGOING STUDIES IN THE field of neuroscience indicate our well-being and happiness is most often determined by how connected we feel to others in our lives. We immediately think of family and marriage relationships as intimate groups in which we feel most connected.

The term "fight or flight" refers to a situation whereby mechanisms in the body are enabled to elicit a rapid and energetic response to threats (real or imagined). This response is automatically triggered in the brain. This is what happens:

- A threat is perceived.
- The autonomic nervous system puts the body on alert.
- The adrenal cortex releases stress hormones.
- The heart beats harder and faster.
- Breathing becomes more rapid.
- The thyroid gland stimulates the metabolism
- Larger muscles receive more oxygenated blood.

Tests show the connectedness we feel for our spouse or other loved ones actually changes the body chemistry to the point where the fight, flight, or freeze stress system in the body is deactivated. It is apparent that our brains are wired in a way that we feel the best when we feel close and connected to other humans. Being connected to marriage partners, family members, and close friends appears to be an important component of being able to live out our mission and vision.

David G. Myers, Professor of Psychology at Michigan's Hope College, concludes from years of research that there are few stronger predictors of happiness than a close, nurturing, equitable, intimate, lifelong companionship with one's best friend.

Real-life Examples

~John Perles

SALLY AND I HAD been dating for a year or so. My life was going great, but something seemed to be missing. I knew what that something was. I wanted Sally to be a permanent part of my life. I didn't want to acknowledge that fact to myself, or anyone else for that matter. Sally had three kids, and I certainly didn't need to tie her up with me, a confirmed bachelor. So, one day I called her and asked her to meet me for lunch. We lived about four hours away from each other.

Sally, with a woman's instinct, knew I was coming to break up with her. As I drove the four hours to meet Sally, I started questioning the decision I was about to make. I decided to mentally list the positives and negatives of our relationship as a way of judging if I was meant to marry Sally. After about an hour of driving, I started to panic, I had twenty-eight items on the positive side and only one on the negative side. The only negative was the fact that Sally was nine years older than I and had three children. It was unlikely we would have children together, which meant I would never have a biological child of my own.

The four hours of driving passed, and there she was, waiting at the park where we agreed to meet. I was in a panic and eventually told her I was very concerned about continuing our relationship because if someday I wanted to have my own children, and if we weren't going to have children together, it would probably end our relationship. I knew what was next; Sally started to cry. I told her I was so sorry I could hurt her in this way. She said she wasn't crying because of us breaking up but because I showed her the respect of honesty and she hadn't had much honesty from others in her life. She agreed that it would be risky to take the chance that I would want my own children in the future, but she was willing to take that risk. Well, I was ready to take that risk, too.

Oh boy ... twenty-three years later we are happily married with six grandchildren that we did have together.

Marriage and Relationships Awareness Review

ACCORDING TO THE US Department of Health and Human Services, research has shown that healthy relationships are crucial to achieving safety, stability, and self-sufficiency. Healthy marriages and relationships require good communication skills, the ability to manage conflict, and financial literacy.

Are you able to answer yes to these statements?

I take responsibility for my own happiness

I make good on my word: I mean what I say; I do what I say I will do

I keep realistic expectations

I listen

Finances Introduction

I believe through knowledge and discipline, financial peace is possible for all of us.

~Dave Ramsey, Founder Financial Peace University

PERSONAL FINANCES ARE AN important, but often overlooked, fact of life. The reluctance to take control of this piece is often rooted in fear or denial. Most of us know how finances impact relationships, lifestyle, and security. Money and planning must go together, or other pieces of your life will certainly begin to fall apart.

Statistics indicate that many marriages fail as a result of poor communication and financial issues. Note this interesting, and worrisome, connection. Money troubles arise, but nobody wants to talk about it! As with all of your other priorities, your financial life must be balanced with the other pieces of your life. The obvious fact regarding financial problems is that, eventually, they will come to light. If you can't pay your bills, it won't be long before you will have to face the fact that you are in deep trouble.

Keeping up with the day-to-day expenses is a basic requirement to keep a family or individual on track. However, it is also important to plan for the future. The matter of retirement may seem far removed from where you are now, but it is never too early to start planning for this event. It can, however, eventually be too late if the matter is given no thought and no action is taken. Take control of your finances and your fate. Follow the strategies offered in this book, delve into the Life Momentum Program, and utilize the tools available to you.

The Brain on Finances

~Amy Guy

THE HEALTH OF YOUR finances impacts your overall physical and emotional health. Financial problems are one of the biggest contributors to stress, as well the number one cause of trouble in marriages. Finances are not just about money. The state of one's financial health is also about security, pride, and avoidance of regret and resentment.

Jason Zweig, author of *Your Money and Your Brain: How the New Science of Neuroeconomics Can Help Make You Rich*, has discovered the following:

- Losing or gaining money is not just a financial or psychological outcome, but a biological change that has profound physical effects on the brain and body.
- Neural activity of someone whose investments are making money is indistinguishable from someone who is high on cocaine or morphine.
- Financial losses are processed in the same area of the brain that responds to mortal danger.
- The amygdala, the area of the brain involved in making financial decisions, is where emotions such as fear, greed, and impulsive behavior originate.
- The prefrontal cortex is where rational decision-making and logical thinking reside.

We need to use both of these parts of the brain to make the best financial decisions for ourselves.

If you make impulsive decisions that impact your financial security, then your amygdala is overactive. If you overanalyze to the point you feel paralyzed, your prefrontal cortex is overactive. In order to make the best, most informed financial decisions, you need a balance between emotion and reason.

Real-life Examples

~*John Perles*

AS YOU BECOME FAMILIAR with the Momentum Wheel, you begin to appreciate how important the principle of balance is to your overall sense of well-being. Occasionally we find ourselves so overwhelmed in one area that other aspects must temporarily take a backseat. Normally this would be a temporary state of upheaval you can deal with using the tools you have accumulated. However, there is one piece of the Momentum Wheel that cannot be ignored for even a short period of time. This is the piece called *Finances*. It is unfortunate when this important piece slips off the radar.

Personal finance, an important life priority, is manageable with awareness and honesty. Procrastination and avoidance merely compound the problems. It is far more difficult to play catch-up and deal with all the ramifications of getting behind than to develop a plan and set goals based on facts.

Dave Ramsey's Financial Peace University, known as FPU, is an excellent source for understanding and planning your finances. The stress and havoc caused by poor handling of finances within a family can be extremely damaging, physically and emotionally. It is credited as the number one reason for failed marriages.

The amount of money one earns is not the issue. Families with comparatively huge sources of income suffer this fate as often as families on a very limited income. It is not the amount of money that is at issue, but rather how that money is managed. One of my clients is living proof of the destruction that comes of poor or altogether-neglected financial planning.

A successful stockbroker, husband, and father well established in his community with an annual income that put him in the top 10% of income earners is now well over one million dollars in debt. He and his wife of twenty-five years are now divorced. When I first discussed his situation with him, he thought he was only $500,000 in debt when in reality he was $1.2 million in debt. He believed he had an earning problem. It was only after we went over his extravagant lifestyle that he realized it was not an earning problem, but a spending problem.

With the track he was on, no matter how great his income grew, it would never be sufficient. Not only was he not aware of his finances, he was not honest with himself or his family regarding their financial situation.

This example may seem extreme. It is not. The phrase "It's all relative" is appropriately used to understand why this experience is fairly common. No matter how much money is available, a little or a lot, it is a limited asset. Denying the necessity to keep track of expenses is a recipe for disaster. Awareness and honesty are the solution to a dilemma that will NOT go away on its own. It is not a sign of failure to find oneself in financial straits, but it is a sign of dishonesty and unawareness to do nothing about it.

Finances Awareness Review

ARE YOU LETTING YOUR financial situation control your life?

What steps are you taking to develop a reasonable, well-thought-out financial plan for yourself?

Ignoring the inevitable doesn't make the inevitable disappear. If you haven't started thinking about your financial life, today would be a good time to start.

HABITS OF FINANCIALLY STABLE PEOPLE:

- They don't spend impulsively, they save money
- They track their spending, and they invest
- They eliminate and avoid debt, and they pay bills promptly
- They give up bad habits
- They plan and take care of their health
- They practice delayed gratification

Community Introduction

Many people are good at talking about what they are doing, but in fact do little. Others do a lot but don't talk about it; they are the ones who make a community live.

~Jean Vanier, philosopher, theologian and humanitarian

WHAT COMES TO MIND when you think of community? Your church, your neighborhood, your town? Community is all of these and more. We think of a group of people living in a specific area. This area might be a neighborhood or a town or a city. Community also suggests a shared sense of ethics and rules by which to live. In other words, community is like family, and family is the backbone of all that comes after. Strong families are the foundation of strong communities.

Working together, sharing and living their values, and exhibiting acts of generosity and kindness are qualities that dwell in a strong family. These are the same qualities found in a robust and successful community. In a family and in a community, it is often the little things that count. Rather than thinking of service to your community as a huge undertaking, realize that small actions can reap large benefits. It isn't necessary to create a foundation or start a fund drive. Search out existing, respected organizations and pitch in to help. Your physical presence may be more worthwhile in the long run to both the organization and to yourself. Families can make a project of seeking out areas in the community that need sprucing up, weeding out, etc. When one person takes on a project, it is a chore; when an entire family pulls together, it might even be fun. Be assured, such actions can also prove to be contagious.

How do you fit into your community? What benefits do you and the community realize with current efforts? Is there more to be done? Working with others can be a great benefit to all. When we share ideas and energy, we all can grow. There is a unique dynamic created when working in a community setting versus a family or business environment.

The bottom line is this: Whether in your personal family or your community family, do a little or a lot, but do something! You'll be glad you did.

The Brain on Community

~Amy Guy

COMMON KNOWLEDGE SUGGESTS, AND scientific research shows, that people are intensely social beings. In his book *Social: Why Our Brains Are Wired to Connect,* Dr. Matthew Lieberman, director of UCLA's Social Cognitive Neuroscience lab, discusses how functional MRI (Magnetic Resonance Imaging) shows how neural mechanisms in the brain cause humans to be social.

Dr. Lieberman's studies indicate the need for humans to connect socially is a basic need in much the same way as are water, food, and shelter. When a person experiences rejection, the unpleasant experience may bring about a sort of social "pain" similar to that associated with physical pain. Contrast that with the feelings of being liked and respected, which activate a neural reward system similar to that of receiving financial compensation.

To view this connection in another way, consider the intense agony a person feels when they lose a loved one. Lieberman argues that, "far from being a design flaw in our neural architecture, our capacity for such overwhelming grief is a vital feature of our evolutionary constitution."

It seems clear, both instinctively and scientifically, that the more we understand our social nature, the more we will be able to improve our lives and the society in which we live.

Real-life Examples

I ALWAYS FELT I didn't have enough time to get fully involved in an unending community project. When I joined Sunrise Rotary, I expected it to be a once-a-month commitment. As it turned out, meetings were held once a week.

I was very uncomfortable attending at first and felt as though I didn't belong. I had the feeling I wasn't good enough or accomplished enough to "really belong" there. But I just kept going. Each week when we would do the Four-Way Rotary Test, it would sink in a little deeper. Before I knew it, I found myself applying the Four-Way Test throughout my work week when faced with something I was unsure about. I also found myself looking forward to going and learning more than I would have ever imagined. Joining Rotary was out of my comfort zone, but it has had a large impact on how I think about things when I am involved with my counseling practice.

~Amy Guy

***

ALMOST EVERY PERSON I have interviewed about their purpose in life has responded that they wanted, in some way, to help their city, state, community, or the world in general. That statement may sound simplistic, but think about it this way. If everyone had that attitude, to be the best they can be, the benefits to themselves and everyone around them would be incredible. Let me give you an example.

Recently, I was reviewing the Momentum Wheel with a Business Momentum client. He expressed concern that he was so busy with his business that he was not actively helping his local community. This gentleman happens to own and operate a very popular restaurant in the community. I asked him how many fundraising dinners he and his staff hosted last year. I asked him how many young people got their very first job at his restaurant. How often had he adjusted an employee's work schedule when family issues arose?

Many of the guests of this restaurant drive in from other parts of the state. As a result, they patronize other local businesses, hotels, gas stations, etc., thereby helping other establishments. The point is, this businessman does a great deal for his community by virtue of the fact that he works hard to create a successful business for himself, his employees, his suppliers, and the community in general.

He felt much better about his contributions to his community by simply looking at his situation from a different angle. He became aware that there are many ways to serve a community. Serving on boards, volunteering for committees, and spearheading social or educational events are admirable undertakings. However, each of us is capable of serving in our own way, as time and talents allow.

Your biggest contribution will come each time you strive and succeed in bettering yourself.

~John Perles

Community Awareness Review

ARE YOU AWARE OF the ways that you can personally benefit when involving yourself in your community?

Volunteering, the act of focusing on someone other than yourself, reduces stress and raises optimism, providing a positive health benefit.

Have you looked at community involvement as a way to expand acquaintances and build networking possibilities? It is also a personal growth opportunity by allowing you to work with people of diverse backgrounds toward a common goal.

When was the last time you involved yourself in a community activity?

Would you consider spearheading a group project for your immediate neighborhood?

What might be a good undertaking that both adults and children could get behind?

Friends, Social, and Fun
Introduction

ONE OF THE BEST rewards for living an organized and balanced life is that time for friends, a social life, and leisure activities are actually built into your days.

Common sense tells us that connecting to other people promotes a positive sense of well-being and belonging. Research backs up this observation. Gallup researchers Jim Harter and Raksha Arora find that people who spend six to seven hours a day socializing tend to be happier people compared to those with little or no social interactions. The type of socializing considered ranges from sharing meals with friends, telephoning a family members, etc. It is the regular interaction with other people, people you enjoy being with or talking with.

As in most things, moderation is best when balancing time with others and time allotted for yourself. University of North Carolina professor Rebecca G. Adams, suggests that a person's well being is impacted by strong friendships; often more so than by family relationships. Professor Adams suggests a need for more empirical study of the importance of friendships.

In order to nurture friendships, one must consciously make time for gatherings or other activities. Stronger relationships serve to create more positive energy. Regularly scheduled get-togethers can be easily logged into your Action Plan.

One of the definitions for the word leisure is "free time". Wow, doesn't that have a nice ring to it. Of course, there is no such thing as free time, but leisure time can be pretty much anything you want it to be. Again, with other pieces of your life plotted on your Action Plan, leisure time is that special gift you give to yourself. Daydreaming comes to mind. It's somewhat of a lost art, but what better way to re-create, imagine, and envision your future than getting lost in your imagination.

The Brain on Friends, Social, and Fun

~Amy Guy

PHD TRAINED NEUROSCIENTIST SARAH McKay knows from her training and client anecdotes that having friends and social connections tends to promote longer and healthier lives. The act of participating in social activities can reduce the harmful effects of stress. Socializing involves cognitive functions, such as thinking, feeling, sensing, and reasoning, all of which aid the brain in maintaining its elasticity.

A variety of leisure activities influence how our brains function as we age. Activities that may include tennis, golf, walking, running, or bicycling keep one physically and mentally fit. Likewise, playing cards and working crosswords or Sudoku puzzles help the brain's synapses fire up and stay active and healthy. The wider the variety of activities you choose, the better you will be for it. The old saying "Use it or lose it" is just as true with brain function as with anything else. Taking up brand new tasks that require learning new skills altogether will help create new pathways in your brain.

The more efficient the circuits of neuronal connectivity, the more your brain can use alternative brain networks. The ease with which the brain can use alternative brain networks improves overall function and makes us better at perceiving an idea in a multidimensional way. The more we train our brains to do different activities that enhance our learning of skills we don't normally use, the more we train our brain to become resilient to age-related decline. The activities we do during our free time aid in our brain's agility to recruit and use several neural networks.

Clearly, the brain is a magnificent organ. The brain actually tells your muscles what to do. It runs your body. So enjoy yourself. Go out and socialize with your friends and have some fun. Maybe you can all learn something new together! Your brain will love you for it!

Real-life Examples

~John Perles

SO MUCH OF LIFE is scheduled with work, family, and other obligations. It is important to mix things up a bit and make sure you are having some fun and relaxation with a little spontaneity thrown in. It is also important to consider time for yourself.

I once asked a friend of mine if he could remember the last time he did something for himself. He was generally occupied with family business matters. He thought for a time and responded that it had probably been years.

My friend was, generally speaking, doing okay, but he appeared to lack real passion and energy about his work, his family, or his life. My question caused him to become aware of just how stagnant his existence had become. Maybe he should try changing things up a bit.

I was encouraged to see that door opening, so I offered my friend a spot on my annual fishing trip. He accepted and invited his father to join us. So it was my dad and me, my friend and his father, and a few other old friends off on a great week of fishing. Twenty years later, my buddy still talks about that trip. He specifically credits the time on the trip as the best quality time he ever had with his father. Overall, he was able to clear his head and recharge his batteries. He continues to join the fishing group on occasion, experiencing the same rejuvenation of spirit each time.

The fun thing about friends, social, and fun is you never know what you are going to get out of it or exactly what's going to happen. It is the one time you can put structure aside, do some creative thinking, open up your mind to new ideas and new experiences, and enjoy the ride.

Friends, Social, and Fun Awareness Review

ARE YOU AWARE THAT having friends is as important to your well-being as much as any other aspect of your life?

It is easy to let your social life be put on the back burner if you don't allot enough time for friends.

Friendships provide valuable support in both good times and bad. Not only do friends provide emotional support, they are often sources for information you may find worthwhile.

How often do you make the effort to arrange a get-together with friends? Do you ever take a few minutes from a busy morning to telephone a friend? These little niceties provide win-win outcomes for both parties.

Spirituality Introduction

None of us knows what might happen even the next minute, yet still we go forward. Because we trust. Because we have Faith.

~Paulo Coelho, Brida

SPIRITUALITY IS A WORD often used to disassociate a person's ideals from any specific religious beliefs. In this regard, faith and trust offer a more universally accepted description to make this distinction.

Faith transcends tradition or doctrine. Faith, though in many ways indefinable, seems an essential quality of being human. Faith comes from an understanding that there is something bigger than ourselves.

We actually know little about the world in which we live, or the universe we inhabit. Faith allows us to function despite not fully understanding all that surrounds us. Faith is trust. Faith allows confidence and assurance to thrive.

Faith and trust instill strength and conviction. Together, they describe the aspects of our existence that give us a sense of meaning and connection. Faith colors our attitudes, our values, and our practices. It influences how we think and how we behave.

The Brain on Spirituality

~Amy Guy

DR. ANDREW B. NEWBERG is the author of How God Changes Your Brain: Breakthrough Findings from a Leading Neuroscientist. Dr. Newberg is part of a research team at the University of Pennsylvania who looks at the connection between God and a person's consciousness. Dr. Newberg posits that the more you think about God, the more you will alter the neural circuitry in specific parts of your brain."

Here are five major conclusions derived from brain imaging work.

1. Different parts of the brain construct different perceptions of God.
2. Each brain assembles its perceptions of God uniquely.
3. Whether a practitioner is a believer or not, spiritual practices enhance neural functioning in ways that promote emotional and physical health.
4. Intense, long-term contemplation of God permanently changes the structure of the parts of the brain that control moods, spatial perception, and sense of self.
5. Contemplative practices strengthen a specific neurological circuit that generates a sense of peacefulness, social awareness, and compassion.

Some of the people I have seen professionally over the years in my practice who have been the most "stuck" and deeply hurt have been ones who have been raised with a strong faith, or attained a strong faith on their own, and then lost their faith. It is as though something very tragic occurred in their lives that caused them to turn away from their beliefs.

Sometimes one event changes their entire view of spirituality and they lose the deep sense of peace they once felt. A client I had counseled for about a year finally came to realize he had lost all faith in something greater than himself when, in grade school, one of his young friends died. Another was a farmer who lost his farmland, the one thing he wanted more than anything in the world. In his despair, he lost all his faith in God.

On the outside looking in, everything may seem the same; but inside, a deep, cold resentment is growing. Often people aren't even aware of the huge impact this has on them. They can give a million other reasons why they are struggling, while the real root of it is their loss of faith.

Real-life Examples

~John Perles

I OBSERVED A FAMILY dealing with challenges related to the parents' separation. In this particular case, the father abandoned his children and all of his parental responsibilities. So where does religion and spirituality fit in this scenario?

To see the confusion, fear, and hurt on the faces of the children was overwhelmingly sad and disturbing. How could this ever be made right? How could any good ever come of this situation? I watched the pain for some time before a friend made a statement. My friend suggested that, even in this dire time, there was still much to be thankful for, even for the man who abandoned his own family.

My friend made the statement that their father is a creation of God and must be accepted as such. This profound statement opened up all kinds of thoughts, emotions, and ideas. Would it be possible to see something positive come out of this anguish? What would it take to bring that about? What would it take to bring about forgiveness? Where would they turn for the healing to begin? How would the injured, the innocent victims of this thoughtless act, eventually become strong and whole again?

It is said that time heals all wounds. This is only partly true. Disappointments and hurts may become numb over time, but real healing begins with true forgiveness and acceptance. Finding the place deep within one's heart and soul to begin this process is, in my mind, a gift from God, man's innate sense of spirituality, or both.

It is by the act of turning over these tribulations to a power stronger than ourselves that we can let go of the anger and disappointment that caused our pain. Miraculously, wounds heal and, in the process, we are made stronger.

Spirituality Awareness Review

IF SOMEONE ASKED YOU how you define faith, what would you say? Does faith play a significant role in your personal life?

The following article was written by Arthur Dobrin, author and educator. It is one person's view on the meaning and importance of faith.

WHY FAITH IS IMPORTANT
By Arthur Dobrin, Professor Emeritus at Hofstra University

Faith is an expression of hope for something better. More than a wish, it is closer to a belief, but not quite. A belief is rooted in the mind. Faith is based in the heart. We act in faith when there is no guarantee, no certainty. No one knows what kind of life an infant will have, yet people continue to have children. No one can know how life with our mates will turn out, yet we continue to have faith our relationships will last a lifetime.

Faith speaks the language of the heart. It is an expression of hope that goes beyond the conscious mind. All that we hold precious rests upon a faith in people, their potential not yet fulfilled. The evidence of history points us in a different direction—the world is full of ugliness, brutality, and injustices. Yet there is also tenderness, kindness and concern and that takes the bigger part of our hearts. Without faith in ourselves we would hold ourselves cheap, and without a faith in others we could never live as free people. This is the water that quenches parched souls.

The Wrap-up

Living Life with Momentum

Daily Living

Words to Live By

Build Momentum by Digging Deeper

Life Momentum Workbook

**Momentum
Builders Inc.©**

Living Life with Momentum

When the finish line seems too far away, remember how you felt when you were back at the starting line. Regain that motivation to recharge your momentum.

~Toni Sorenson

NOW, AS WE COME to the end of *Your Life Is Your Business* and the Life Momentum program, is a good time to take stock of how far you have come in developing your momentum-building skills. You have been given the tools necessary to deal with challenges and opportunities in all aspects of your life.

We trust you enjoyed this process and will continue to benefit from the skills you have learned through this program. It should be clear to you now that Life Momentum is built on the premise that humans are capable of so much more in life than they realize. Life Momentum calls upon each of us to be aware of this concept, equip ourselves with the appropriate tools, and develop a blueprint to move from where we are to where we want to be.

To live your life to its full potential is the most critical goal in honoring your mission. Do not let yourself get caught jumping from one of life's challenges to another, ignoring the connectedness of the various aspects of your life. Choose to address the entire Momentum Wheel as you work your plan, realizing your full potential and gaining momentum toward your dreams and goals.

The same core principles that guide great businesses to long-term success are applicable to both you and me. You now have a powerful business plan for your own life. Your mission statement identifies your purpose, and your vision statement gives you direction by identifying your dreams and aspirations. Your Action Plan assists you in turning your dreams into reachable goals. Look at your Action Plan and give yourself a pat on the back. You are more aware, more organized with a well-prepared plan than 99% of the people on this planet. Your efforts reflected on the Action Plan have set you up to be more successful, more energized, and more prepared for the challenges and opportunities yet to come.

Life, as business, is about incremental improvements. Keep going. Never stop learning or growing or planning or dreaming. The tools we've introduced to you will serve you well for the rest of your life.

Daily Living

~Amy Guy

TAKE TIME EACH MORNING to form an idea of how many hours in the day you plan to spend on particular aspects of your life. Perhaps you want to devote at least two hours catching up on your finances, paying bills, reviewing your budget. Your child's after school activities require your presence. You will need at least one hour for that. The luncheon meeting with your community outreach group will last about ninety minutes. Mentally apportioning the hours of your day to fit with your responsibilities for that day will put you in charge of how you spend your time.

You will be amazed at how much time you really have at your disposal once you begin to utilize this tactic. During the course of any day it is important to schedule what can be called Internal Time. Living—as most of us do—in a fast-paced environment, we need quiet, reflective time more than ever. Remind yourself you are a human being, not a human doing! Just BE for five or ten minutes in each day. Pause and pay attention to what is happening in the moment.

When you eat, focus on what you are eating, not what you are going to do after you finish eating. You will find your Internal Time allotment to be time well spent. It's a time to recharge, reaffirm, and regenerate. As you literally stop what you are doing and focus on your breathing, you will find you are able to calmly sort through the many thoughts swirling in your mind. As with any new exercise, it will take time to establish your Internal Time regimen, but the rewards are worth the effort.

Getting physical exercise, to whatever extent you are able, must be factored into your day as a "must do" activity. It is best to plan your exercise regimen for the same time every day. It is well documented by health care professionals that physical exercise, along with a healthy diet, is the cornerstone of a healthy mind and body.

A wonderful way to end a day is to engage in the practice of gratitude. Research provides evidence that practicing gratitude has positive effects on our physical health, our psychological well-being, and our relationships with others. Many families have the custom of saying grace before a meal. Similarly, you can simply reflect quietly on several things for which you are grateful.

For those who keep a personal journal, the act of writing down some of the things they are grateful for in life is beneficial. It provides a tangible reminder of the many parts of life to be appreciated.

Build a better world said God
And I asked how?
The world is such a vast place and so complicated now
I am small and useless
What can I do?
God in all His wisdom said, "Just build a better you."

~Anonymous

Build Momentum By Digging Deeper

HAS ANYONE EVER TOLD you to use your head? Well, if they did, they were giving you some excellent advice, because inside of your head resides the most amazing machine imaginable.

As you read through *Your Life Is Your Business*, you came across a number of articles about the brain. In each case, I attempted to impress upon you the intricacies and the importance of this wonderful organ. In addition, I hoped you would be intrigued enough to want to learn more about the brain.

We are fortunate that in this technological world, information of every stripe is literally at our fingertips. And because this modern technology is user friendly, most of the information you come across is clearly stated and easy to understand.

Digging Deeper encourages you to seek out additional information on the various topics introduced in *Your Life Is Your Business*. A printable Life Momentum Action Plan Workbook is ready for you to look at right now on the following pages. To print out this version, follow the simple steps indicated below.

To download an online Life Momentum Action Plan Workbook, available at no charge to readers of *Your Life Is Your Business*, follow the simple instructions shown below.

1. Go to

   http://momentumbuildersinc.com/registernow/
2. Register serial number 24682468A
3. Select either the printable action plan workbook, or the online action plan.

~John Perles

Acknowledgments

The publication of *Your Life Is Your Business* is the result of a life spent in the quest of knowledge, understanding and a commitment to the belief that each of us is more capable than we realize. My association with Amy Guy was instrumental in providing scientific research findings for the ideas I instinctively believed to be so. Amy's thoughtful input continues to affirm the validity of my vision to bring this message to an increasingly wider audience.

Kudos to my daughter for suggesting I take on the monumental task of putting my ideas and goals in book form. Kelli's encouragement and prodding kept me focused and on task. Sally, my wife, my helpmate and my sounding board, supported me in this challenging endeavor with patience and optimism.

No project can succeed without a support team. My book creation and launch is no exception to this rule. Jamie Palmer, Outlier Marketing, dragged me, kicking and screaming, into the world of modern technology. My mother had the daunting task of improving my syntax in her role as editor. Paige Duke and Alexander Hemus, Standoutbooks.com, managed to make this dream a reality.

To my special friends go my special thanks. A lifelong mentor, Sally Forbes, has been a guiding light and steadying hand in all areas of my life. To Doc Joe, Sharon Hartmann, Bob Hicks and Craig Lindvahl, goes my appreciation of their honest feedback and true friendship. From my father I learned the importance and joy of a job well done and the treasures to be found in family and friends.

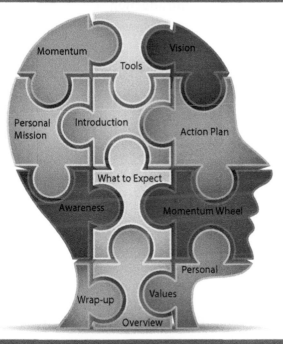

Momentum

Vision

Tools

Personal
Mission

Introduction

Action Plan

What to Expect

Awareness

Momentum Wheel

Personal

Wrap-up

Values

Overview

LIFE MOMENTUM
WORKBOOK

Momentum
Builders Inc.®

My Life Momentum Action Plan
The Difference between a Dream and a Goal is a Plan!

Introduction
Familiarize yourself with the Action Plan

Action 1: Personal Mission Statement
Write your Mission Statement below (see pg 12 for help)

Action 2: Personal Vision Statement
Write your Vision Statement below (see pg 13 for help)

Action 3: Personal Values Statement
Write your Personal Values Statement below (see pg 14 for help)

I live my life with these values in mind:

1. **Honesty**
2. **Awareness**
3.
4.
5.

Action 4: Momentum Wheel

Fill in the areas from 1–10 to indicate your current level of awareness in each of the pieces of your life. Number 1 would indicate least satisfied, number 10 most satisfied.

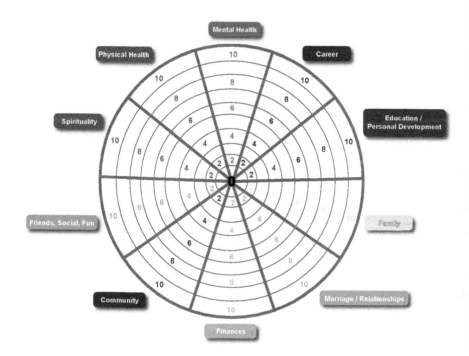

Action 5: Momentum Wheel 10-Piece Exercise

PHYSICAL HEALTH

Write in detail where you are with your Physical Health.
Your weight, your strength, medicines, illnesses...

Write where you want to be, your vision for your Physical Health.
Healthy, diet, strong, fit, lose 10 lbs...

Write an affirmation regarding your Physical Health.
I eat healthy, drink 8 glasses of water per day, and exercise 3-4 times per week.

Write 2 actions you can commit to that will help you move from where you are to where you want to be with your Physical Health.
1) weigh myself   2) check my blood pressure   3) drink 8 glasses of water/day   4) give up alcohol/ soda for a week   5) take care of any symptom that I have been ignoring

MENTAL HEALTH

Write in detail where you are with your Mental Health.
Anxious, stressed, on edge...

Write where you want to be, your vision for your Mental Health.
Calm, able to handle stressful situations...

Write an affirmation regarding your Mental Health.
I am full of energy and vitality and my mind is calm and peaceful..

Write 2 actions you can commit to that will help you move from where you are to where you want to be with your Mental Health.
1) spend 30 minutes alone each day   2) write in diary daily   3) eat 3 meals per day   4) connect with others, make phone call or lunch date
5) 3 things I like to do: schedule time to do them   6) learn how I deal with and react to stress

Action 5: Momentum Wheel 10-Piece Exercise

CAREER

Write in detail where you are with your Career.
Good job, good work relationships, highly regarded...

Write where you want to be, your vision for your Career.
Promoted to new position or new job...

Write an affirmation regarding your Career.
I am a valued person at my workplace and my voice is always heard respectfully.

Write 2 actions you can commit to that will help you move from where you are to where you want to be with your Career.
1) Take Continuing Education courses to raise my value as an employee   2) Look for openings within my company to be promoted

EDUCATION / PERSONAL DEVELOPMENT

Write in detail where you are with your Education/Personal Development.
Books currently reading, classes to take...

Write where you want to be, your vision for your Education/Personal Development.
New courses taken and results achieved, reading one book/month

Write an affirmation regarding your Education/Personal Development.
I love gathering knowledge and studying comes naturally to me.

Write 2 actions you can commit to that will help you move from where you are to where you want to be with your Education/Personal Development.
1) Take 1-2 personal growth courses per year   2) Read one book a month

Action 5: Momentum Wheel 10-Piece Exercise

FAMILY

Write in detail where you are with your Family.
Spend good quality time...

Write where you want to be, your vision for your Family.
Good communication, family meetings scheduled, spend quality time...

Write an affirmation regarding your Family.
I hug my children daily and demonstrate my love in other ways as well.

Write 2 actions you can commit to that will help you move from where you are to where you want to be with your Family.
1) Plan 2 Family outings per month   2) Schedule weekly family meetings

MARRIAGE / RELATIONSHIPS

Write in detail where you are with your Marriage / Relationships.
Spend quality time, good communication...

Write where you want to be, your vision for your Marriage / Relationships.
Married, good communication, trust, vacation together...

Write an affirmation regarding your Marriage / Relationships.
I love my spouse. Daily quality time is a priority in our relationship. Our communication is honest and respectful.

Write 2 actions you can commit to that will help you move from where you are to where you want to be with your Marriage / Relationships.
1) 2 Date Nights per month   2) Take a walk together twice a week

Action 5: Momentum Wheel 10-Piece Exercise

FINANCES

Write in detail where you are with your Finances.
In debt, college savings...

Write where you want to be, your vision for your Finances.
Savings Plan in order, life insurance set up, kids college savings set up

Write an affirmation regarding your Finances.
I am aware and in control of my income and my expenses. I plan responsibly for my financial future.

Write 2 actions you can commit to that will help you move from where you are to where you want to be with your Finances.
1) Go over budget and figure out how to save $400/month that can go to savings   2) Meet with Financial Planner to get Money Markets set up

COMMUNITY

Write in detail where you are with your Community.
Volunteer work, valuable member...

Write where you want to be, your vision for your Community.
A leader in the community, contributing member

Write an affirmation regarding your Community.
I am aware of living in a community and am aware of my impact.

Write 2 actions you can commit to that will help you move from where you are to where you want to be with your Community.
1) Volunteer for a community fundraiser that means something to me   2) Join a community board

Action 5: Momentum Wheel 10-Piece Exercise

FRIENDS / SOCIAL / FUN

Write in detail where you are with your Social Life.
Good friends, fun healthy hobbies...

Write where you want to be, your vision for your Social Life.
Better relationships, more meaningful activities...

Write an affirmation regarding your Social Life.
I appreciate every moment of the day. Learn from good and bad experiences is my motto.

Write 2 actions you can commit to that will help you move from where you are to where you want to be with your Social Life.
1) Plan a quality group activity once a week with good friends   2) Start a book club

SPIRITUALITY

Write in detail where you are with your Spirituality.
Are you a spiritual being? Daily prayer / meditation...

Write where you want to be, your vision for your Spirituality.
Closer relationship with God, daily meditation or prayer...

Write an affirmation regarding your Spirituality.
My spiritual growth benefits my life and the lives around me.

Write 2 actions you can commit to that will help you move from where you are to where you want to be with your Spirituality.
1) Commit to going to church weekly   2) Daily prayer

Action 6: Life Momentum Action List

Reference the Momentum Wheel 10-Piece Exercise if you need help.
Write the action with due dates on your Action List below.

Daily Actions	Notes on Specific Action
Review Action Plan™	Take 10 -15 minutes each day to review your Action Plan
Give 3 Gifts	Give someone a big smile. Tell someone you love them. Hold a door open for someone.
Read your top 3 Affirmations	Bring your top 3 affirmations up from the Momentum Wheel 10-piece exercise and read them daily.
Affirmation 1	
Affirmation 2	
Affirmation 3	

Action List: List the Action Items from your 10-Piece Exercise

Daily Actions	Notes on Specific Action	Date Due

Action 7: Continue Working Action Plan Daily

Mission Statement

Vision Statement

Values Statement

Daily Actions	Notes on Specific Action
Review Action Plan™	Take 10 -15 minutes each day to review your Action Plan
Give 3 Gifts	Give someone a big smile. Tell someone you love them. Hold a door open for someone.
Read your top 3 Affirmations	Bring your top 3 affirmations up from the Momentum Wheel 10-piece exercise and read them daily.
Affirmation 1	
Affirmation 2	
Affirmation 3	

Action List: List the Action Items from your 10-Piece Exercise

Daily Actions	Notes on Specific Action	Date Due

Action 1: Mission Statement Reference Page

Personal Mission Statement: My purpose, reason I exist

Pick one of these Sample Mission Statements or adjust one to make it your own.

Dr. Joseph Hartmann, Cardiologist: Live long, live well.

Oprah Winfrey: To be a teacher. And to be known for inspiring my students to be more than they thought they could be.

Sir Richard Branson: To have fun in my journey through life and learn from my mistakes. I find enjoyment in my personal life through traveling and finding new places to explore. I find opportunities to use my natural talents and gifts such as art, being a good friend, a creative thinker to help others around me.

To work creatively, to grow, to build with reason as my guide.

To honor my abilities, God, and my family and to positively influence families.

To be a positive example of a full, happy, well-lived life.

To live in a way so that my actions inspire others to improve their lives.

Work on your Mission Statement below.

When you are satisfied with your Mission Statement, write it on your Action Plan.

Action 2: Vision Statement Reference Page

Personal Vision: My dreams, aspirations and goals

Pick one of these Sample Vision Statements or adjust one to make it your own.

To be a great parent to my three children, a supportive spouse, and to be happy and fulfilled in my journey.

I am strong, healthy and fit. I am pain free and able to work creatively and joyfully in my role.

To live a balanced life. To be financially secure by fifty and have a career I will stay in for the rest of my life. To have success that necessarily benefits me and those around me.

My foundation builds schools in Africa where there are none to help spread my message to young girls.

I am a cardiologist and a loving, active parent. I am trusted and enjoy helping others with all things medical.

I joyfully do work that profits both my pocket and my soul. I am energized traveling to amazing places, spending time with wonderful and diverse people and sharing knowledge.

Work on your Vision Statement below.

When you are satisfied with your Vision Statement, write it on your Action Plan.

Action 3: Values Statement Reference Page

My Statement of Personal Values

Sample Value Statement:
I live my life with these values in mind: Honesty, Awareness, Accountability, Confidence, Enthusiasm

Words to consider in creating your Personal Values Statement:

Awareness	Commitment
Passion	Mindfulness
Change	Vision
Growth	Timeliness
Honesty	Open Mindedness
Accountability	Trust
Confidence	Making A Difference
Consistency	Thoughtfulness
Reason	Persistence
Responsibility	Adventurous
Effectiveness	Enthusiasm

For additional sample words, refer to Steve Pavlina:
http://www.stevepavlina.com/articles/list-of-values.htm

Work on your Values Statement below.

When you are satisfied with your Values Statement, write it on your Action Plan.

Issues and Ideas Dump

The first step is to empty your mind of the many issues that are bogging you down by writing each one on a Issues and Dumps. Review the list and select one or two of the easiest projects to accomplish. Do not carry more than one or two action items in your head at any one time. Dump the rest on your action plan. You will establish a pattern of prioritizing which will help you in all areas of your life. The key is to employ the Issues and Ideas Dump on a regular basis and add to your momentum building tools.

Momentum Wheel Rating Chart

	CURRENT	1 MONTH	2 MONTHS	3 MONTHS	4 MONTHS
Physical Health					
Mental Health					
Career					
Education/Personal Development					
Family					
Marriage/Relationships					
Finances					
Community					
Friends, Social, Fun					
Spirituality					